CW00407199

Ayahuasca:
A Beginner's Guide

How to Prepare for Your Ceremony

by

Derek Dodds

Copyright © 2023 by Derek Dodds

Cover Art by Kate Cleaves | www.katecleaves.com

About the cover: Jaguar is a gatekeeper to the mystical and awakens our soul to its real purpose and power. The jaguar challenges us to face fears and meet barriers head-on. Jaguar embodies a superior vision revealing hidden aspects of ourselves cloaked by darkness. Jaguar brings pristine clarity that leads to the lucidity of self.

The content contained within this book may not be reproduced, duplicated, or transmitted without direct written permission from the author or the publisher.

Under no circumstances will any blame or legal responsibility be held against the publisher, or author, for any damages, reparation, or monetary loss due to the information contained within this book, either directly or indirectly.

Legal Notice:

This book is copyright protected. It is only for personal use. You cannot amend, distribute, sell, use, quote, or paraphrase any part, or the content within this book, without the consent of the author or publisher.

Disclaimer Notice:

Please note the information contained within this document is for educational and entertainment purposes only. All effort has been executed to present accurate, up-to-date, reliable, and complete information. No warranties of any kind are declared or implied. Readers acknowledge that the author is not engaged in the rendering of legal, financial, medical, or professional advice. The content within this book has been derived from various sources. Please consult a licensed professional before attempting any techniques outlined in this book.

The plants and compounds mentioned in this book are illegal in many countries, and even possession can carry severe criminal penalties. None of this book constitutes medical advice or should be construed as a recommendation to use psychedelics.

By reading this document, the reader agrees that under no circumstances is the author responsible for any direct or indirect losses incurred as a result of the use of the information contained within this document, including, but not limited to, errors, omissions, or inaccuracies.

Awaken Publications

www.awakenpublications.com

Library of Congress Control

ISBN-13: 979-8-3886-7375-6

Spiraling Toward the Tea

Spiraling upward, the Phoenix can foresee
the struggles of you and me

beyond life's marquee
is a secret—don't you agree?

sacred myths hold the key
follow the dance of the bee

life is god's potpourri
not a spending spree

wake up and drink the tea
from the spiritual tree

take a trip to your inner Waikiki
your soul is the designee

your childhood trauma is the VIP
plant medicine is the referee

get on one knee
prayer and gratitude are love's sea

there is a fee
if you flee

your life is not leftover debris
don't be a spiritual absentee

is your soul trapped in ghee
like a dried-out pea

make a plea
to simply be

my beloved thee
he, she, and we

all creatures, I decree
are designated trustee

your heart deserves jubilee
and your soul is meant to be free

~ Derek

Table of Contents

Dedicated to the spirit of ayahuasca, indigenous people, and all my medicine brothers and sisters.

~ Derek

Introduction

Ayahuasca is a healer.

The word heal comes from the Old English word *hǣlan*, itself of Germanic origin, which means to "restore to sound health." This is precisely what ayahuasca does. It restores health while healing the broken parts of ourselves. However, this healing does not come easily. Ayahuasca reveals the pain and sorrow buried deep within the psyche and allows us to meet it head-on. Only through this direct relationship with our pain can we ignite our healing energies to move back toward sound health.

I spent several decades of my life entombing my trauma. My pain was enveloped in a cocoon deep inside my heart, and I locked away the butterfly key of freedom. My pain manifested in addiction and psychological turmoil. I ran from myself and hid in the superficial sunshine of adventure and physical sensation. I never acknowledged that I needed help, nor did I want to look weak—even though inside, I was screaming for support.

In 2015, my mother died, and something shifted deep in my being. Some Indigenous tribes suggest that we are energetically connected to our mother's umbilical cord. My mother left me at age two and never really returned. She did try to reconnect with me at the end of her life, but I couldn't find the strength to start again. This seed of sorrow in my heart blocked my ability to feel real love, and I learned to shield my heart from emotion and pain.

After my mother's death, the energetic cord around my heart loosened. My healing journey started with books and podcasts. I spent time learning about trauma and asking my dad about my childhood. I began to piece together the cryptic puzzle that was my early life. I was pulled toward a pilgrimage of healing that led me back to plant medicine. My healing started gradually with psilocybin, and I started to see a psychologist once a week. After several years of laying this foundation, I was called to a transformative year where I sat in a ceremony with ayahuasca more than twenty times in twelve months. My friends and family challenged my path. "You are going again?" they would frequently ask. I felt judged. I couldn't explain my actions to my rational self, and it took strength to wade through the criticism of those around me. I was being pulled by something mysterious. I was ready to answer the call.

Western culture has traditionally used medicine to treat superficial wounds of the flesh and psyche. However, ayahuasca works on a deeper level. Ayahuasca heals the soul and releases deep traumas and pernicious ancestral energic patterns attached to our etheric bodies. The etheric body is part of our energetic field and is attached to our physical form. Thus, anything that influences the etheric body will also appear in physical form. Clearing or releasing negative energies from the etheric field can bring deep healing to the physical body.

Ayahuasca is a magician.

I have heard it said many times by both participants and teachers, "Ayahuasca is magic." Before taking ayahuasca, I never believed in magic, and I still cannot explain many things that happened to me during ceremony. I remain skeptical yet open. Christian Funder said it well in his book *Grandmother Ayahuasca*: "[Ayahuasca] reveals that the mind has almost cosmic proportions, and to try to explain exactly what will happen upon ingestion of this plant medicine would be a fool's errand."

One of my teachers frequently says right before ceremony, "I have no idea what will happen." After sitting over twenty times in one year, I can wholeheartedly report that it is always different. Ceremony is never what you expect it to be. As we say in the plant medicine world, ayahuasca gives you what you need, not what you want. As Don Jose Campos said in the book *The Shaman and Ayahuasca*, "Once when I drank Ayahuasca, she very gently explained to me, she told me, 'Look, I give to you, but I take away.' So I insisted, 'What do you give me? And what do you take away?' She said, 'I take away defects, and I give you responsibilities.'"

The plant has a spirit. I don't know what that even means, but it feels right to say it. I've learned this year that my relationship with the plant has evolved. I have come to honor and respect my connection to ayahuasca, and I feel a kinship building as I dance with her. She is a living entity, embodying the magical spirit of the jungle and cosmos. She is introducing me to myself through myself and restoring my ability to connect with the divine. I know that's a big word, and I don't use it lightly, but it's the best way to describe what is happening.

Ayahuasca is powerful and mysterious, and the more gratitude and humility I bring to her, the deeper my healing is. I am still learning to open a conversation with her, pray to her, ask her questions, and praise her power and wisdom. I know it might feel strange to speak with a plant, but she listens and wants to communicate.

Ayahuasca is a teacher.

All great teachers ignite something deep within us. They remind us of our potential, and they model a holistic way of being. Good teachers move us closer to wholeness, and they help us deconstruct our trauma and rebuild bridges to our open hearts.

Much of our inner wisdom lies dormant in the shadows of our being, hidden behind our childhood wounds. Our superpowers lie just behind these wounds, and the healing starts once we hold ourselves up to the truth and allow the light of clarity in. Ayahuasca shoots an arrow of fire into our wounds and helps us start the process.

Ayahuasca dissolves defense mechanisms and cracks our hearts open, allowing grief and sadness to be felt. It's an arduous journey, and it requires a warrior's courage. Ayahuasca is not for everyone, but when it is for you, you will know it because she will call you to her side, and you will not doubt your path. It happened to me suddenly, and it could also happen to you. As said by both Buddhists and Theosophists, "When the student is ready, the teacher will appear."

Ayahuasca is a therapist.

Ayahuasca is benevolent, and she is merciless. Ayahuasca understands that real healing reveals the obscurity in our souls' darkness. Some people fear ayahuasca not because she creates scary hallucinations but because she exposes the ugliness of our past behaviors and holds us accountable to the truth.

People say that one night of drinking ayahuasca is like ten years of therapy. For me, it's been a wonderful supplement to other work (including therapy, breathwork, cold therapy, exercise, and healthy eating) that I was already doing in my life. Ayahuasca is like a therapist, but it doesn't replace therapy. We are complex beings, and working with a therapist may help you in ways you never thought possible. If you mix plant medicine and therapy, I suggest hiring a therapist or coach with personal experience with psychedelics.

Ayahuasca pulls nuggets of self-knowledge into the light, but she does so like a warrior tearing a sword out of a wound. Most therapy is gentle; it takes time and requires a commitment to regular sessions. Ayahuasca is more direct. The naked soul both rejoices and quivers at ayahuasca's sight. The soul recognizes that the heart is the doorway toward joy, and ayahuasca helps open that door and allows us to regain the throne of love's kingdom. May she call you back to your throne.

The History of Ayahuasca

To drink yagé... is to return to the cosmic uterus and be reborn. It is to tear through the placenta of ordinary perception and enter realms where death can be known, and life traced through sensation to the primordial source of all existence.

~ *When Plants Dream,* Daniel Pinchbeck and Sophia Rokhlin

Ayahuasca isn't a recent discovery. Nobody knows how old ayahuasca is or when Indigenous tribes started using it. The Amazonian tribes that currently grow and use ayahuasca do not have written records of their origin, and thus we can only speculate about ayahuasca's legacy.

However, there is mention of a mystical potion used in the Indian Rigveda from 1500 BCE. These sacred texts suggest an ayahuasca-like substance called "Soma" was used to enter into spiritual rapture. In Rigveda VIII.48.3-4, it says:

> We have drunk the Soma. We have become immortal. We have reached the Gods. We have entered the realm of heavenly light. What now can the ungrateful do to us? What harm of the mortal, O immortal Soma? Grant peace in our hearts when drunk, or dropped. Gracious as a father to his son, a friend to his friend, wise and of good counsel, O Soma, extend our lives for our souls.

If you replace the word Soma with ayahuasca in that paragraph, it accurately describes the experience of an ayahuasca journey.

While we have a lot of anecdotal evidence regarding ayahuasca ceremonies, it's essential that we approach them with an open heart. It's important to understand the plant's spirit and its benefits. We also need to know how the ceremony is traditionally performed, how it has gained popularity in the West, and why it's crucial to respect its origins. Once we're aware of these aspects, we need to prepare ourselves for the ceremony to receive the maximum benefits from it.

This book is meant to be a guide for your first ayahuasca ceremony. In each chapter, I will reveal lessons and techniques I learned by working with many ayahuasca teachers. But first, let's get to know this psychedelic drink better.

What are Psychedelics?

Psychedelics are a class of substances that can alter our minds and consciousness. Classic psychedelics disrupt neural activity by diffusing through the brain and activating a serotonin receptor known as the 5-HT2A receptor. Psychedelics alter our mood, perception, and consciousness in ways that can otherwise only be experienced in certain dream states or through religious practice, trance, meditation, and deep breathing. This state is not easily achieved, and its effects are transformative. Psychedelics help awaken a connection to Source energy and let us drop the psychological baggage of the ego connected to trauma and low self-worth.

Psychedelics don't cause users to become overly dependent on them. Compared to other drugs, there is almost no chance of getting addicted to them. These substances have shown promise in treating various mental conditions such as anxiety, depression, and addiction. While research is still underway regarding these compounds, initial evidence has given a lot of hope to people in the mental health research community.

Of course, this hasn't always been the case. When we pay attention to the terms used to describe these substances over the decades, we get a sense of how the scientific community has perceived them. In the 1960s and 1970s, most scientists referred to these substances as *psychotomimetics*, which indicates that these drugs could mimic the symptoms of psychosis by causing delusions or states of delirium. This wasn't a positive term, and it presented these drugs as something to be avoided.

Later, the term *hallucinogens* became more popular, but even this didn't do any justice to their full range of properties. This is because these drugs don't produce hallucinations all the time or if taken in controlled doses. Also, these terms don't discuss their benefits or potential in any other way. In 1957, a psychiatrist named Humphry Osmond coined the term *psychedelics*. This phrase has Greek origins and translates literally to "mind-manifesting." This term tells us something about the capabilities of this class of compounds and talks about its immense potential when used judiciously. That being said, many scientific community members have resisted using this term because of its positive connotations.

There have been concerns about using psychedelics for recreational purposes in healing and therapy, and the U.S. government has echoed these concerns. In 1970, it passed the Controlled Substances Act, which placed all psychedelics into the most restrictive category of drugs. Schedule I drugs are those substances that don't have any known medical benefits and have a very high probability of being abused. When this law was passed, it became virtually impossible to research psychedelics and their healing properties. President Nixon's war on drugs drove psychedelics into the closet for several decades, and it appears humanity is waking up to a new psychedelic paradigm as I write these words.

In the last few decades, there has been a growing body of research, especially concerning psilocybin (a naturally occurring psychedelic compound found in magic mushrooms), which shows that we might have underestimated the effect of psychedelics in healing and therapy. These studies are gaining popularity, and we are entering a new era of psychedelic acceptance by the medical community. The fact that tightly controlled studies by reputed institutions and laboratories are being sponsored and given credence by the scientific community gives us hope for the future. In many ways, psychedelics are seeing a resurgence in the collective consciousness, but this time in a positive manner.

Researchers and scientists caution against excessive enthusiasm regarding psychedelics because we still have a long way to go toward establishing these substances as appropriate for widespread use. Yet the future looks promising. After twenty years of working with plant medicine, I propose that this medicine is what humanity needs to heal in a time of disconnection and disassociation.

What is Ayahuasca?

Ayahuasca is a plant-based psychedelic tea that different Indigenous groups in the Amazon have traditionally brewed. Also called *iowaska, yajé, yagé, vegetal, natema*, *uni*, or *caapi* (depending on the different regions and cultures where it's used), it's made from the bark and stem of the *Banisteriopsis caapi* vine, along with other ingredients.

There are at least two parts involved in the making of this tea. The first one is the vine, which doesn't have psychedelic properties. It's a source of an alkaloid called harmine (which acts as a monoamine oxidase inhibitor, or MAOI), which prevents the main psychoactive ingredient (DMT) from breaking down in the digestive tract. This way, DMT can reach the bloodstream and the brain, allowing us to experience its psychedelic properties. The stems and bark of this vine are usually boiled with the second ingredient, the leaves of *Psychotria viridis*, *Psychotria carthagenensis*, or *Diplopterys cabrerana*. These plants contain the psychoactive component responsible for the psychedelic properties of ayahuasca.

Ayahuasca has been used for centuries by First Nations peoples from contemporary Peru, Brazil, Colombia, and Ecuador for religious ritual and therapeutic purposes. I am so grateful to these communities for sharing ayahuasca with the world and giving the West access to this medicine.

Let's take a moment to give gratitude to First Nations peoples.

Etymology and Significance

Even though the West has appropriated these ancient traditions, the word ayahuasca gives us a hint regarding its origins and significance. It belongs to the Quechua language, an Indigenous language family spoken by people residing in the Peruvian Andes. In Quechua, *aya* means "soul" or "spirit", and *wasca* stands for "rope" or "vine". Ayahuasca is the "Vine of the Spirit" or "Vine of the Dead."

This term tells us how sacred the vine and its properties are considered to be by the Indigenous. Besides the various (usually pejorative) terms that have been used to describe psychedelics over the years I mentioned earlier, there's another term that changes the perception of these compounds entirely: *entheogens*. It's a neologism rooted in two Greek words, *entheos,* and *genesthai*. While *genesthai* means "to come into being", *entheos* translates to "being full of God". We can substitute the word God for Source, creation, cosmic energy, creator, the divine, higher self, grand spirit, or any other words that fit our worldview.

Fifteen years ago, I had a dream that I was writing the phrase "Enthusiasm is the essence of life" over and over on a chalkboard. I was both writing the phrase and sitting in a child's chair, taking notes. Though I understood the dream, I didn't feel it in my heart until I took ayahuasca. Very similar to entheogens, enthusiasm means to be inspired by Source. That dream was trying to tell me that the essence of life is to be inspired by something greater than myself. Ayahuasca offers a similar lesson.

The word *entheogen* describes ayahuasca perfectly, and it is the word I encourage you to use when describing or thinking about this medicine. However, I'll continue to use the word psychedelic in this book since it is more commonly known. These compounds ignite the sacred through healing, divination, artistic development, and other spiritual activities. Words are powerful. Words formulate the world we live in. Choose the words that empower your experience and bring you closer to Source.

Origins of Ayahuasca

As indicated earlier, ayahuasca has traditionally been used in healing and divination ceremonies by the Indigenous tribes of the Amazon. This includes people in Ecuador, Peru, Columbia, Bolivia, and Brazil, among others. A shaman guides and bridges the material and spiritual worlds in these ceremonies. Visions often serve as paths to healing various mental, emotional, and physical illnesses. As rich as these traditions are, they were largely unknown to the Western world for a long time.

Introduction to the West

Around the 19th century, this narrative began to change. Many explorers and ethnographers were interested in the Amazon basin and wanted to understand its people's customs and traditions. Fascinated by what they saw, many stayed with these Indigenous tribes for long periods, observing things the West had no understanding of at the time. Chief among these mysteries was the use of ayahuasca in ceremonies. While their accounts mentioned the drink and the vine it came from, they were sparse in their details.

This changed in 1852, when the English botanist, explorer, and ethnographer Richard Spruce first found ayahuasca being used in a ceremony among the Tukano people. These people were primarily based along the Vaupés River in Brazil. After witnessing the ceremony, he decided to travel along the Amazon to find more ceremonies like this. In the next six years, he encountered these ceremonies among the Guahibo people in Venezuela (who chewed the bark instead of making the brew) and the Záparo people along the border of Ecuador and Peru (where he learned the name ayahuasca). He soon realized that this plant was growing almost everywhere along the Amazon basin.

At the same time, he understood that this plant had a great spiritual significance to Indigenous people. It was important for him to depict this sacred relationship in his accounts. In 1873, he published a book called *Notes of a Botanist on the Amazon and Andes*, which became the first ethnobotanical account of ayahuasca to be available in the West. In this book, he elaborated on the sources from which the drink was made, how it was prepared, and its effect on him.

Along with Ecuadorian geographer Manuel Villavicencio, who, in 1858, wrote about the use of ayahuasca in a divination ceremony among the Shuar people, this book remained one of the earliest accounts of ayahuasca ceremonies in their native settings. Spruce was also responsible for collecting vine specimens and naming the Banisteria caapi, later renamed *Banisteriopsis caapi* in 1931. He sent these specimens to his country to be tested, where they were found to be psychoactive.

Popularization in the West

Ayahuasca took a long time to become the phenomenon it is today. This was mainly because the scientific community and the government approached these plants with wariness. The counterculture movement that gained steam in the 1960s and 1970s brought psychedelics into the limelight, and the government created a propaganda campaign that framed psychedelics as unsavory and dangerous. This paranoia made no distinction between the drugs, their properties, and their uses. Ayahuasca also bore the brunt of the ban on using and researching these compounds.

It took a body of pioneers, often called psychonauts, to bring these compounds back into the public consciousness. The more sophisticated psychonauts realized that the only way these substances could find widespread acceptance was through a body of research backed by credible organizations. This is why scientists and researchers made extensive efforts to get government bodies and reputable research institutions to fund their clinical trials and experiments.

One of the most important studies was headed by psychiatrist Rick Strassman in the 1990s. In these studies, he decided to delve deep into the effects of the DMT molecule on the participants. It took him two years to gain the approval of various institutions to conduct these studies at the University of New Mexico. The results were revelatory and astonishing. While Hungarian chemist Stephen Szára had tested DMT on himself in a clinical setting in 1956, this was the first time the effects could be seen in a larger group of people.

Between 1990 and 1995, healthy volunteers took high doses of DMT and recounted their bizarre and transformational experiences afterward. These experiences were recorded in the book *The Spirit Molecule: A Doctor's Revolutionary Research into the Biology of Near-Death and Mystical Experiences*, published in 2000. This book, along with the hugely popular 2010 documentary it inspired called *DMT: The Spirit Molecule*, brought ayahuasca to the forefront of public consciousness. By 2007, Strassman had co-founded the Cottonwood Research Foundation, which investigates the effect of psychedelics on human consciousness.

In 1998, anthropologist Jeremy Narby published a book called *The Cosmic Serpent*, based on his experiences with the Asháninka Indigenous community in Peru. In this book, Narby spoke of the many ways in which ayahuasca influenced Indigenous knowledge. He believed that this knowledge predated scientific discoveries made in the West.

For example, Narby believed that these communities knew about the double helix shape of the DNA molecule and referred to it as the *twin snake* symbol. He also believed that shamans could use ayahuasca to accurately diagnose patients and even visualize the specific plant that could cure their particular illnesses. In other words, ayahuasca formed the basis for science and medicine in Indigenous societies.

This book was seen as groundbreaking research into Indigenous cultures because it combined science, anthropology, spirituality, and culture. Together, these books and documentaries were responsible for the growing popularity of ayahuasca in the West. We owe much gratitude to these early psychedelic pioneers for their contributions.

Ayahuasca Ceremony Origins

While it's believed that this vine was used in Indigenous traditions almost 5,000 years ago, there is little concrete evidence to support the claim. Other sources believe that while some ancient rituals used the vine, they did not use it in ceremonies until much later. Since no archaeological or written evidence supports these claims, most anthropologists are intrigued by two main questions about this plant.

First, they are interested in understanding how Indigenous cultures discovered the plant. Second, since they had no scientific method for determining the effects of ayahuasca on their psyches, how did they use it for ceremonial purposes? Other questions of particular interest also relate to the lack of sources that mention ayahuasca use in these communities.

For example, the Incas of Peru—who ruled over most of South America until 1,400 CE—and the Europeans who colonized South America in the 1500s never mentioned any use of ayahuasca in their reports. This is despite the fact the Incas were known to be avid botanists and had immense knowledge regarding Indigenous plants. On the other hand, the Europeans wrote about other psychoactive plants but never about ayahuasca.

This could mean that either the plant itself (or its uses) was an incredibly well-kept secret or that the ceremonial use of these plants as psychoactive substances started much later than previously thought. While the smoking or inhaling of plants containing DMT has been recorded as far back as 900 BCE, no evidence suggests it was made into a psychedelic brew.

Many shamans claim that the knowledge needed to combine the two vines and make the brew was given to them through dreams and visions. In other words, it's believed that the vine itself chose the communities it wanted to commune with. Others claim that the brew was discovered by accident and was used more widely once its astonishing properties became known.

The consensus among anthropologists is that the use of ayahuasca as a ceremonial tea began hundreds of years ago. Still, the traditions that form the basis for these ceremonies are thousands of years old.

Adoption by the West

Along with the work of Richard Spruce and Jeremy Narby, it was the work done by Richard Evans Schultes and Albert Hofmann in their 1979 book called *Plants of the Gods* that prompted many influential figures in the West to take part in Indigenous ayahuasca ceremonies. This included writers like Allen Ginsberg and William S. Burroughs, who later wrote accounts of these experiences.

Many people have started going to the Amazon basin for these ceremonies in the last few decades. One reason is that the substance is completely banned in the U.S. and most Western countries. Another reason is that people want to experience these ceremonies in traditional settings.

When it comes to the Indigenous communities themselves, some feel that having foreigners spend money on these ceremonies can be a good deal for them. However, many others believe that people who don't belong to the communities that understand the vine on an intimate level should not be allowed to participate in ceremonies. Various churches have started using ayahuasca for mystical or divination purposes and have skirted legal restrictions. You may be able to join one of these churches in your area to circumnavigate the legalities.

The situation, as you can imagine, is complicated. However, many foreigners have started training under *ayahuasqueros* to understand precisely how these ceremonies are conducted. These shamans believe that they must teach these people the correct methods of using this vine in ceremonies. In some ways, this is a way to ensure that the ceremonies held in the West are as authentic as possible.

Respecting the Vine

This section will address the impact our current interest in ayahuasca has on Indigenous communities. I believe that before we embark on this journey, we should understand what this vine means to the societies where it has been used traditionally. While everyone can benefit from its transformative properties, we should respect the context in which this vine is used and the communities who share this sacred knowledge with us.

Most Westerners don't have a sacred relationship with Pachamama like many Amazonian communities do. Many of the rituals performed in these communities don't have a parallel to our own. It takes some time to feel into the ceremonial space. When I first started attending the ayahuasca ceremony, I always wanted to get something from it—"What is in it for me?" is a common mantra of our culture. But something shifted when I realized that the ceremony was an active prayer, an opportunity to gather with my brothers and sisters in communion.

Much of the music rooted in these ceremonies comes from the Indigenous communities of the Amazon. The music played in most of these rituals has a deep meaning for the shaman. *Icaros* are traditional songs played during ceremonies that offer reverence and protection. These songs carry the life force of each shaman who performs them and the magical energy of oral traditions passed down for generations. The ceremony is a prayer. Be mindful of the song lyrics during the ceremony, and let them penetrate your heart as you listen to each note.

It's true that we might want to have these experiences for spiritual or therapeutic reasons, but these ceremonies are a part of the traditional culture of many communities. It isn't simply something they do for a day or two; they are immersed in these sacred conversations with ayahuasca and other plants.

In a later chapter, we'll discuss the importance of choosing a proper retreat for our experience. While one reason for this is that we should ensure that the guides are properly trained, the other is not blindly believing anything they might tell us.

There have been instances where tricksters posing as shamans have made people participate in activities that have nothing to do with the ceremony itself. Since we don't know what happens in these ceremonies, we might believe people are trying to dupe us or even abuse us. Not all Amazonian communities are related to ayahuasca ceremonies. This is why it's essential to understand a shaman's lineage.

We can't understand all the intricacies of these ceremonies, nor can we be completely sure of their authenticity.

None of these things mean we must stop using ayahuasca or participating in ceremonies. There are very real benefits to the use of this vine. However, we should always treat these cultures with respect, understand these traditions, and approach these ceremonies with honest intentions. We might experience some things in the way that Indigenous communities do. That's ok.

Ayahuasca ceremonies are evolving, transitioning, and changing as they move out of the jungles and into our culture. Some shamans are very traditional, and others are more creative. I suggest you sit with a few teachers and find the style most resonates with your heart. As you heal and your relationship with ayahuasca changes, the teachers you sit with might also change.

Ayahuasca will lead you where you need to go. Surrender is an essential pillar of this journey. Surrender to the divine (and the vine), and she will take you to places you have never imagined. As my teacher Natascha said recently in our ceremony, manifesting into the unknown is a decisive surrender of trust and magic.

One

Meeting the Vine

A woody vine is mixed with leaves from a bush to create a concoction that the native shamanic people believe can set the soul free from corporeal confinement—allowing the soul to roam free and visit other realms that are not bound by space or time.

~ *Grandmother Ayahuasca,* Christian Funder

Now that we understand what ayahuasca is and its origins and use in ceremonies let's discuss the benefits and possible side effects of consuming this psychedelic brew.

How Does Ayahuasca Affect the Brain?

In the clinical sense, ayahuasca causes hallucinations within 30 minutes of being consumed. However, people who have consumed other psychedelics, like LSD, believe that the visions or experiences associated with this brew are more spiritual and mystical. Therefore, most people who participate in ayahuasca ceremonies don't do so for recreational purposes (though there might be some exceptions).

Research on Ayahuasca

While we still need much more research on how ayahuasca affects the brain, some studies have been conducted on this topic. For example, a 2018 study published in Frontiers in Neuroscience investigated how DMT can regulate brain function and how it shows promise in treating mental illnesses (Barker, 2018).

One of the most promising areas of this research is the effect of ayahuasca and other psychedelics in the treatment of those mental illnesses which have shown resistance to conventional methods. Researchers believe that these psychedelics can affect neural activity so that they can change how we express emotions and think and behave.

Most brain imaging studies want to establish a connection between the effects of psychedelics like ayahuasca on the default mode network (DMN). This brain area activates when the mind is at rest or disengaged from the outside world. When the DMN gets overly active, it can lead to excessive rumination and anxiety about the future. It's also been linked to the ego, which means that when we spend too much time thinking about ourselves (not self-reflectively but in an obsessive manner), we tend to get depressed.

Now, experts say that psychedelics have a calming effect on DMN; in other words, they can help reduce frenzied activity in the brain. Since this area is believed to have ties to addiction disorders as well, there is a lot of promise in treating depression, phobias, and addiction disorders using psychedelics like ayahuasca.

Since ayahuasca is said to impact the brain's limbic system and visual cortex, it can directly impact how we process memories and emotions. This results in many vivid images shown to us when we consume ayahuasca. These memories contain details of our past and traumas that we might have kept from ourselves. When we see these memories resurface in visions, we are profoundly affected by them.

In 2016, a paper in Frontiers in Pharmacology aimed to delve deeper into the therapeutic effects of ayahuasca. According to the results, the two main conclusions of the paper were that ayahuasca might be beneficial in reducing chronic inflammation in our bodies. We need to understand the benefits of ayahuasca solely from a biological or scientific perspective (Frecska et al., 2016). These conclusions are interesting for a variety of reasons.

For one, the reduction of chronic inflammation through the use of ayahuasca would be a great find for several reasons. Inflammation occurs in our body when we have an infection. This is usually due to the immune system getting signals to fight off an infection. Sometimes, our immune system malfunctions and becomes overly active. In such a scenario, inflammation occurs without any trigger. While acute inflammation can be resolved in a short duration of time, chronic inflammation is usually lifelong.

Inflammation has been linked to various diseases, including autoimmune disorders, chronic pain, and cancer. This is why this study offers hope.

I have had direct experience with ayahuasca's healing potential. I have suffered from psoriasis since childhood. Psoriasis is an autoimmune disease that causes lesions on my body that sometimes itch and are uncomfortable. Ayahuasca helps keep the inflammation under control, and my skin is mostly clear of psoriasis after ingesting this magical brew.

The second part of the conclusion states that a truly comprehensive account of ayahuasca can only be made if we consider its biological, social, psychological, and spiritual effects. This is a significant step forward in the understanding of psychedelics, especially plant-based entheogens. When a scientific paper gives credence to the spiritual aspects of a psychedelic, it shows an increase in the acceptance of these compounds for therapeutic and spiritual purposes.

Another review of the research being done in the field of psychiatry was published in *Current Neuropharmacology*. It concluded that the research conducted by various scientists indicates that ayahuasca can be used to treat various mental disorders. Regarding side effects, the research shows that the effects are mild and not too worrying; however, more research with larger groups is needed. Another significant point noted in the paper was that more researchers in the scientific community are keen on the relaxation of government laws regarding psychedelics. By this, they mean that it should be easier for scientists to research the therapeutic effects of ayahuasca on people with mental disorders (Hamill et al., 2019). Again, this indicates that the scientific community's attitude is changing concerning ayahuasca and other psychedelics.

While it might be too soon to rejoice, the future looks promising for psychedelics and ayahuasca.

Before going into ayahuasca's physical and psychological effects, let's talk about set and setting. When scientists started to gain an understanding of the properties and effects of psychedelics, two things came into sharp focus. It was understood that psychedelics do not work on their own. While they have inherent properties that can induce similar effects across multiple individuals, the individuals themselves can profoundly affect how these psychedelics work.

Set refers to a person's state of mind when consuming the drink. This would mean that their mood can significantly impact how ayahuasca affects them. If you have certain expectations regarding how the ceremony will go, your experience will also be moderated by those expectations. This is true even if you have had previous experiences with ayahuasca or other psychedelics. If you go into a session with feelings of fear and anxiety, chances are that your actual trip might justify those feelings. Similarly, if you've previously seen spectacular visions on a psychedelic trip, you will also be influencing your subconscious during this experience. This is why much emphasis is placed on understanding the psyche of anyone who wants to participate in a session or ceremony. This is especially important in clinical trials, but it might impact the participants even in spiritual ceremonies.

Setting refers to the environment in which the psychedelic is being consumed. Where are you participating in the ceremony? Is it a closed or suffocating space? Is it a small but cozy room? Is it in the great outdoors? Who are the people with you? Do you trust your surroundings? Do you trust your guide? Do you feel safe enough to be vulnerable? Is the environment calm and peaceful, or is it too noisy? What kind of music (if any) is being played? All these affect your experience. Your environmental conditions don't need to be overt; they can be extremely subtle things like the vibes you get from a place. This might seem weird to someone outside this experience, but these energies matter when dealing with spiritual forces. Even in clinical settings, therapists go to great lengths to ensure that the participants feel calm and centered before the studies begin.

I can't over-emphasize how important the setting is to your experience. Everything is energy, and if the container you are stepping into for the ceremony is polluted, it will harm your experience. I am already sensitive to public spaces, and I can feel the energy—ayahuasca magnifies this sensitivity. Ideally, I look for a place that is a sacred temple or that is in nature. Visit the place before the ceremony to 'feel into' the energy to determine if it's right for you. If something feels off energetically, find a new location.

Effects of Ayahuasca

The effects of ayahuasca vary widely according to the amount taken by the participants, the strength of the decoction, and the effects of the other plants or substances being used. Even a person's size, weight, and physical health might modulate the effect of ayahuasca. Additionally, some people metabolize the ayahuasca slower than others, so don't be surprised if the effects hit the person next to you more rapidly.

The most widely accepted psychological effects of ayahuasca include

- having stronger emotions than usual that are mostly related to your past experiences;

- experiencing intense visions—which can be related to our own experiences or feelings or can be intensely spiritual or mystical;

- a warped sense of time and space;

- feeling your consciousness expand and getting closer to the Universal Consciousness;

- moving through or reliving childhood traumas and processing past traumatic experiences to heal.

The visions, if experienced, don't necessarily have to be visual. Sometimes, these visions are related to the music that plays in the background, various additional sounds experienced by us, or a message we are meant to hear. It's believed that many people lose their sense of time and space and feel they have accessed a higher dimension. It's not uncommon to have a conversation with the spirit of ayahuasca—like a teacher, she can illuminate an aspect of our journey and bring clarity to our lives.

Benefits of Ayahuasca

There are numerous benefits. For one, ayahuasca is a great spiritual teacher. When we come out of an ayahuasca experience, we find ourselves more spiritually inclined. We tend to have greater respect for the unknown and believe that their energies are affected by those that don't exist on the material plane. This is frequently referred to as the unseen world. Before I started my journey with ayahuasca, I had very little connection to this dimension of life, and now I feel great respect and connection to the spirit world. The important thing is to remain open and curious—nobody is asking us to shift our beliefs—however, ayahuasca does open us up in mysterious ways.

When we are more spiritually connected to ourselves, we tend to feel a sense of calm and an anxiety reduction. We understand that there's more to life than the struggles we usually concern ourselves with. This doesn't mean that we begin to have delusions of grandeur (though we should always check for that), but rather that we understand something about our higher purpose.

When we experience spiritual energies around us, we feel protected on our path, and we have faith that life will work out for us as long as we are true to ourselves. This can also help us let go of any wounds or pain we have been holding on to and experience a spiritual cleansing. Visions happen when we're meant to have them. Remember that ayahuasca gives us what we need, not what we want—use these visions to help shape your spiritual journal and let them guide you toward more profound meaning and connection to yourself and the divine.

Witnessing mystical phenomena feels like our worldview has been changed for the better. Not only do we feel more connected to the forces in nature, but we also develop the courage needed to make significant changes in our lives. It's said that it takes an event as significant as a near-death experience for us to start thinking about life differently. Many people don't live authentically until it's too late. This experience can seem as significant as birth or death to the participants. It might even be seen as a renewal or rebirth in many ways.

While mystical phenomena are wonderful, they aren't very common. Far more common is the effect that ayahuasca has on our mental, social, and emotional health. Ayahuasca increases focus and concentration in some participants, which means we stay on task and become more productive. It can also be extremely effective in helping us deal with our past issues and trauma. Many people who suffer from depression, PTSD, and addiction disorders have experienced a positive impact from taking ayahuasca.

People who suffer from chronic pain, or those dealing with terminal illnesses, often feel that life has become meaningless. Some feel numb; some are perpetually exhausted, while others feel disconnected from everything around them. Ayahuasca can help ease chronic pain and make us feel calmer about our impending deaths. Participants say they feel more accepting of their fate and want to spend more time with their loved ones. Some people even see death as a beginning rather than an end. While these effects are psychological, they couldn't be possible without the spiritual aspect of these ceremonies.

An exciting facet of ayahuasca that sets it apart from LSD or psilocybin is that the people who witness hallucinations or visions during these sessions are aware of themselves being in this state. This brings a whole new level of awareness to the entire experience. Perhaps this is why people come out of the ceremonies with extreme awareness of their issues and traumas.

While there are a lot of benefits to taking ayahuasca, it also comes with specific side effects. Even if most of them are mild or rare, we should still be aware before committing ourselves to the ceremony.

Physical Risks of Ayahuasca

Usually, ayahuasca does not have adverse physical effects on people. By this, I mean that there are no significant changes in our major organs because of this substance. While some changes might be observed in the immune system, these are not long-lasting and don't affect our health in any manner. However, it can cause an increase in our body temperature. It's also been known to affect our blood pressure and heartbeat, so people with severe cardiovascular concerns should avoid taking ayahuasca.

The most common side effects that people have during the ceremony are diarrhea and vomiting. Also known as purging, this indicates that our bodies are ridding themselves of any impurities, whether physical or spiritual. However, too much vomiting and diarrhea can cause serious problems, including extreme dehydration and nausea.

In certain rare cases, people can faint during the ceremony. While it's unclear why this happens, it might be due to physical exhaustion (if the ceremony is intense) and purging (which can leave us feeling weak). Therefore, it's important to ensure people don't get hurt in the unlikely event of fainting.

Certain medications should not be taken during an ayahuasca ceremony, which will be discussed in a later chapter. Your teacher will ask you for an intake call, or they will request that you fill out a release form detailing your current medical condition. If nobody talks to you about your medical condition or medications before your first ceremony, I would avoid that teacher and community and find someone else to facilitate your first ceremony.

Psychological Risks

While most accounts of ayahuasca, under both clinical and ceremonial conditions, have good things to say about the experience, you must understand that each experience is intensely personal. As mentioned earlier, your state of mind and previous experiences with psychedelics (if any) will play a role in your experience.

When undergoing a hallucinatory episode, you will usually feel emotions such as fear and anxiety taking over. You might even feel paranoid sometimes, but these effects are usually temporary. Also, when our hidden traumas resurface, they're bound to bring some discomfort to them. In extremely rare cases, these effects can be prolonged. Some people call these experiences *bad trips*, in which their anxiety, confusion, and paranoia can spiral out of control. However, my view is that a *bad trip* is simply your fears being exposed and your inability to face those fears with an open heart, gratitude, and kindness. Ayahuasca reveals those aspects of ourselves that are difficult to acknowledge and process. Revelation is the first step toward healing.

Apart from hallucinations, you might also have to deal with depersonalization. During an episode like this, you might feel like you're stepping outside your body to observe yourself from a distance. Again, these scenarios, including a loss of time and space, are not uncommon. Most people are conditioned to expect all this. However, how these effects manifest within you can differ significantly from anything you've read or heard about. This is why choosing your retreat center, and facilitator wisely is essential, which we will discuss later.

You must exercise an abundance of caution if you have a history of mental disorders. I know there have been promising studies in therapeutic research using psychedelics, but these studies are small in scale and too few to come up with conclusive results. When you decide to participate in a ceremony, you need to understand that mental conditions can complicate matters. In some cases, your symptoms might disappear, only to reappear later in your life. In more extreme cases, your problems might be exacerbated. Again, these instances are rare, but you must understand that these things are possible.

When it comes to long-term effects, studies have not shown any adverse effects on the body, neither in physical nor psychological terms. Frequent use of ayahuasca is common in some communities, and the results have been positive. The Santo Daime groups suggest drinking ayahuasca every two weeks for the greatest benefits. Participating in ceremonies every six to eight weeks could be a remarkable cadence. There is no right or wrong answer here. Follow your heart, and it will lead you toward the optimal path.

Now, it's time to prepare for the ceremony.

Two

Preparation

It is important to understand that one is not ingesting a liquid, one is ingesting the spirit of the plant. One then acquires the mariri [protection and healing] and one advances spiritually. With the plants the process of spiritual advancement is accelerated.

~ *The Shaman and Ayahuasca*, Don Jose Campos, Geraldine Overton, Charles Grob, and Alberto Roman

While you might be raring to go and ready to have your first-ever transformational meeting with the vine, there are a few things to keep in mind. Since this is a psychedelic brew that has been a part of different cultures in the Amazon for a long time, it's important to understand how these ceremonies are conducted traditionally. This will give you a sense of what to expect when you finally participate in the ceremony.

Even more important is to understand that many of the experiences we're about to have in the upcoming ceremony are deeply spiritual. The vine itself is considered to have sacred properties. It's safe to say that most of us aren't adequately prepared for the experience we're about to have because we're not rooted in the same environment as most of the original communities in the Amazon.

As with any psychedelic, ayahuasca also places great importance on *set* and *setting*. This means that our experience will be influenced by both our environment (social, cultural, physical) and our personality and mood at the time of the ceremony. Therefore, we need to prepare ourselves for the experience beforehand.

Before we begin discussing the different preparations we need for the ceremony, let's discuss the environment in which we want to participate in the experience.

Choosing the Right Set & Setting

In the previous chapters, we've discussed how the West has adopted the traditional ayahuasca ceremonies differently. While some of these retreats like to keep the ceremonies as close as possible to the original ones, others put their spin on it or modify certain aspects to suit their audience. Both styles can offer wonderful experiences. As I mentioned, try a few teachers before committing to any tradition or group.

When discussing traditional ceremonies held in Amazonian cultures, we have too many differences to treat them all as one. Not only are the leaders or guides of these ceremonies given different names, but they also have different roles depending on where the ceremony is being held. Research beforehand is a good idea if you're going to Peru or Brazil for your ayahuasca experience. Ideally, you will be able to speak with someone who has been to a specific retreat center or has sat in a ceremony with a particular group. First-hand experience from someone you trust is always the best form of recommendation.

If you're attending a ceremony in the West, you might have concerns regarding their legitimacy or intent. Again, find someone you trust to recommend your first experience or ask a friend to join you on the journey. A friend can offer a sounding board as you research various teachers or retreat centers. When I returned to ayahuasca after a decade-long absence, I asked my childhood friend Clarke to join me. We both researched retreat centers together and selected the right teacher and location for both of us. His support and advice were crucial in making the right decisions on that initial internal voyage.

Let's first understand the three broad categories that these ceremonies fall into:

- **Religious sessions**: Some churches use ayahuasca for religious purposes. Most of these churches have their roots in Brazil, and the most important ones are Barquinha, Santo Daime, and União do Vegetal. The rituals in these churches vary according to the church, but their members usually take ayahuasca two to four times each month. There are strict rules regarding how one should behave during these sessions. While these ceremonies are predominantly religious, there is room for spiritual and philosophical work. Of course, this depends on the religious leader leading the session.

- **Shamanic ceremonies**: The original ayahuasca ceremonies were almost exclusively shamanic. This means some guides led the participants on a spiritual journey and had a very important role in these ceremonies. For example, there were *curanderos*, also known as healers or *vegetalismos*, who knew the sacred knowledge contained in plants. Traditionally, these guides needed to be immersed in Indigenous knowledge and rituals to conduct these ceremonies. During the ceremony, they would blow tobacco smoke on participants, cleanse the space, and lead the participants using music or singing. The instruments and music differ according to the country the session takes place. Usually, the shamans also have assistants who help the initiates with various issues they might face during the sessions. Even today, many places try to stay true to their roots and perform these sessions with as much authenticity as possible.

Many people have trained under these guides in the West and now perform these ceremonies themselves. They are known among some groups as neo-shamans, but this is a misleading word. For me, there is nothing "neo" about these teachers; they are shamans through and through. Most of these ceremonies are deeply spiritual. Even though healing can be an essential part of these experiences, the main aim is usually to have mystical encounters or get closer to the Divine Source in whatever form that might manifest for us.

- **Therapeutic sessions**: These sessions are usually held in Western settings and are a result of the growing number of studies that have been conducted on the therapeutic properties of psychedelics. Needless to say, these sessions should only be held at legitimate facilities where there's a certified therapist present. Also, it's the norm for such sessions to have proper preparation and integration phases for the participants. How these sessions play out depends on the therapist conducting them. They usually pay special attention to the setting in these cases, which means you might have the option of listening to soothing music or staying in a room that has been carefully decorated to ease your mind. There are many things to remember while holding these sessions, especially since the participants might already suffer from certain mental conditions, such as depression or anxiety.

Even those who are otherwise psychologically healthy might take part to understand themselves better and improve their quality of life.

There are some other things to keep in mind. Since most religious churches belong to a close-knit community, one can expect that those who regularly participate in these experiences might be taken care of afterward. In shamanic sessions, too, there might be an element of integration, though it might not be as structured as in therapeutic settings. Again, it's essential to understand the context of where these sessions are taking place. The intention with which you participate in them is extremely important, but you still need to be open to whatever you might experience along the way. There are religious ceremonies that might also be deeply spiritual. Similarly, a therapeutic experience might occur alongside a mystical one. Your experience with the medicine will likely change with time. My experience started therapeutically and has morphed toward spirituality.

Now that we have a general idea of the different sessions, let's go through some other points you need to remember before choosing a retreat or ceremony for yourself.

Choosing the Right Setting

You must decide between the many centers across South America and the West. There are several factors to consider when deciding which place is appropriate for you. Some people believe they can only have true ayahuasca experiences in their origin. There are two concerns here. One, not all of us have the time or resources to fly to another country and stay there for an extended period. Two, since there has been an exponential growth in the number of people *seeking the vine*, there's no reason to believe that all the centers there will be legitimate and honest. There might be a greater chance of falling for tricks in the name of authenticity. This doesn't mean you shouldn't go, just that you should do your due diligence in the same way as you would anywhere else. Another thing to consider is the cultural and linguistic differences.

You might feel a little nervous if you're going for your first ayahuasca experience. This is to be expected. Most good centers understand this and take care of their participants. However, if you want a rawer experience and work with shamans in smaller communities, you have to be prepared because they might not communicate with you as quickly as in the West. There's no right or wrong choice here. The only thing to understand is that your setting matters and your chosen place is vital.

Some other questions should inform your decision:

- **Are you particularly interested in an experience with an Indigenous person, or would a well-trained Westerner do?** Some "neo-shamans" are exceptional at what they do, and they are very keen on keeping the ceremonies as authentic as possible.

- **Are you looking for a primarily religious, shamanic, or therapeutic experience?** Remember that each of these ceremonies will be very different from one another. Especially when it comes to religious ceremonies, you might find them a bit more unsettling and strange if you don't have any religious context for them. This doesn't mean you can't try them out, but you should have some idea before going in. Again, these sessions will have undertones of other types of sessions, but you must consider your primary intention when attending them.

- **What is your level of participation in these ceremonies?** Some people, especially first-timers, may want to observe the shaman doing their work, while others find it more effective if they are an active part of the sessions. Would you prefer the shaman to lead in singing, dancing, and other rituals, or would you also want to participate? This is also connected to the kind of group you're a part of. Would you want to be part of a vast or smaller group? How intimate would you want the ceremony to be (keeping in mind that more co-participants might put your mind at ease)?

- **Are you particular about certain things related to the ceremony space?** For example, do you want to be in a place that allows you to sleep over and rest after the ceremony but isn't necessarily luxurious? Or would you prefer a retreat that has more amenities and resembles a resort? Also, would you prefer that the ceremony be held indoors in a specific room, or would you rather be outdoors? Is it important for you to be connected at all times, either by being in a proper city or having access to the internet or would you rather be in a remote location that is cut off from the hustle and bustle of daily life? Some of these questions might seem trivial or even superficial, especially considering that you're looking for a spiritual rendezvous with a sacred plant. However, these things might matter more to you after the ceremony. For example, if you're someone who usually suffers from trust issues because of specific heartbreaking and dangerous experiences you've had in the past, you might be worried about the level of vulnerability you reach during these sessions. Knowing that you have a secure, private room waiting for you instead of a more public sleeping arrangement might help you to be calmer during the experience.

Be honest with yourself, and don't worry about your choice. However many people sit with you for the ceremony, you will have a unique experience. Always keep that in mind when making these decisions. Your decision will be the right one you need at that very moment. Source is here to support us. We are served exactly what we need every moment to help raise our vibration.

Choosing the Right Person (Shaman)

I have used the word "person" instead of "shaman" or "therapist" because the name, as well as the role of the facilitators, changes depending on the kind of session and its context. This guide is a very important part of your journey and can decide how the ceremony goes for you. If there's anyone you are placing your trust in, it's them. Trust your intuition and follow the recommendations we mentioned earlier.

These are some questions you should consider:

- **What is the background of the shaman?** Where do they come from, what are their beliefs and cultures, and how long have they been doing this work? All of these things will influence how they perform a session. If you're working with a therapist, you should still be sure of their credentials and approvals for working with ayahuasca in therapy. This is especially important if you go to these ceremonies to get help with depression or PTSD.

- **Is the shaman trained?** If so, how and by whom? You might think this doesn't make sense, but again, there have been instances where people conduct ceremonies without sufficient knowledge regarding the work that needs to be done for support and guidance. Some people only administer the medicine and step in when needed. This might work for a participant who has experience with many ceremonies, but even then, it's not advisable. There's a reason that shamans perform a lot of labor during the ceremonies. The singing, dancing, and other rituals aren't for show. When your guide is deeply involved with you in the process, it makes you feel safe and cared for and affects the quality of your experience.

- **What is in your brew?** When dealing with a psychoactive substance, it's essential to know how much of it you'll be taking, what goes into your drink, and how strong it is. One of the things about ayahuasca is that its effects are not extremely long-lasting, but you will still need to know if the decoction is extremely strong. Another thing to remember is that some ceremonies use other substances, such as kambo, tobacco, or rapeseed to facilitate the process. This doesn't mean anything suspicious about it; many traditional ceremonies use them regularly. What's important is that you should be aware of this. The same goes for the process of administering these drinks. Do you have to take everything that is offered to you? Do you have a say in it, or do you have to surrender yourself to the process completely? Is it a one-time administration, or are there multiple rounds throughout the ceremony?

- **How does the shaman work?** Do other healing or spiritual methods work together with the ceremony? For example, some shamans also work as healers and have experience using limpia therapy or reiki to help the participants during the sessions. Limpia therapy is a spiritual cleansing technique where the healer tries to remove the negative energy or toxicity that might be stored in the participant. They usually do this through a massage. Reiki is a Japanese form of energy healing where the healer uses their hands to transfer positive energy to the patient. This way, they free them from any concerns, anxieties, or other issues plaguing them. While these are beautiful alternative therapy methods, some people might want something other than that level of involvement their first time. Others might see it as proof that they will get a well-rounded experience.

- **What is the level of engagement between the participants and the facilitators?** Some centers may want to avoid anxious people hounding them before the ceremony has even begun, but there should be a channel of communication established beforehand. Can participants ask questions and meet the healer before or after the session? Are there enough assistants to take care of you during and after the experience? This is especially important to consider. While there are traditional ceremonies where the movement of participants might be less restricted, it's crucial to understand that these ceremonies are part of their culture and daily lives. This is not the case for most of us, so we want to ensure that we are in good hands even after the ceremony.

- **What are the criteria for working with people with prior medical or psychological concerns?** Some people expect to find relief from chronic pain, anxiety, depression, and even pain related to cancer. Some suffer from chronic heart conditions or hypertension. While they might find relief through these ceremonies, there is also a concern regarding how these issues might affect, and be affected by, the ceremony itself. So they'll want to find a therapist who works with these conditions. In any case, you need to inform them about your medical history. Specific centers might not accept you based on your condition, but quite a few will. Finding a safe space for yourself in any situation is vital.

Some other things to ask about regarding the ceremony include: What do you need to bring for the ceremony? What are the preparations you must do before it takes place? What does the integration process look like? In a later chapter, we'll discuss the integration process in greater detail, but in general, this process helps you make sense of the experience you've just had. While there's no one way this experience will play out for everyone, there are specific methods by which we can come out of the experience feeling supported and encouraged on our healing or spiritual journey.

Also, inquire about the referral process if you want to direct other people to the facility. Remember that ayahuasca is still banned and illegal in many parts of the world. While exceptions are made for religious and therapeutic purposes, you must ensure your experience is as discreet as possible. When facilities advertise their services or have testimonials from customers under their original names, think twice about the legal aspects of such operations.

Before we move on to our preparation for the ceremony, one last thing to remember is that the best places are transparent and objective when providing information. Taking ayahuasca can be an emotional and scary experience because we're not used to that level of vulnerability or connection with ourselves. Therefore, we need people who will be honest with us about what to expect and the potential concerns surrounding the experience. We wouldn't want to interact with someone who sounds like a salesperson or is in any way insincere.

Places that are clear about their screening process (and that have a good screening process in the first place), that conduct interviews with participants before and after the ceremony, and who have been referred by people you can trust are the best choices.

Preparing Yourself for the Ceremony

You need to be prepared for the ceremony to benefit from it and reduce the chances of anything untoward. Most of the time, there is nothing to worry about regarding these ceremonies. However, this is the *set* part of the experience. Your own prior life experiences, your social conditioning, and even your physical and psychological state during or before the ceremony will affect how the ceremony plays out for you.

In many Indigenous communities, the preparation done by shamans before their first (or each) ceremony is incredibly intense. Since most of those sessions are conducted to commune with the Divine, the preparation for them is taken seriously. The word traditionally used to describe the preparation process is *dieta*. I like to think about this period as a cleansing of our body, mind, and soul. We cleanse and prepare our vessel so that the spirit of ayahuasca has a beautiful place to dance and play.

The Importance of Dieta

In Spanish, *dieta* refers to diet. However, when we speak of this word in the context of experiences with the sacred vine, it becomes broader in scope. Dieta refers to any physical, social, or psychological preparation you must make to commune properly with the plant. In the Amazon basin, this doesn't just refer to experiences with ayahuasca but also deals with healing, consultations, divinations, and even hunting. Whenever the human being comes into close contact with the plant world (which is considered sacred and intelligent), *dietas* are used to facilitate the experience and to show our reverence toward the unseen world.

In traditional societies, plants are considered a part of our lives. While this differs from Western ones, there are good reasons to follow many of the instructions that form a part of these preparations. Shamans who have been practicing these rituals in the Amazon are traditionally made to isolate themselves as part of a *dieta*. They can spend days, weeks, or even months in the deep Amazonian jungles, living in a spare cabin and eating foods that have symbolic significance to the ritual. These usually include fresh fish and animals found in the jungle, cassava, and plantain. There are some peculiarities about where the ritual is held, but sex and alcohol consumption is strictly prohibited almost everywhere.

In the Western world, there is usually a much longer list of things to avoid, and we will go into the reasons for that shortly. However, some might find these restrictions extreme and unnecessary. Whenever we have a profoundly therapeutic or mystical experience, we connect with energies that either don't exist on this plane or are buried deep within us. These subtle energies lie behind a thin veil inside ourselves, and the *dieta* helps us prepare for a deeper connection to this part of our individuality.

If you are otherwise healthy (physically and psychologically), ignoring the *dieta* will only create a few problems. However, I recommend you stick to the *dieta* and prepare for the sacred ceremony. If you decide not to follow the *dieta*, you will have an uncomfortable experience physically (especially in terms of vomiting), and those toxins left inside your container might not mix well with grandmother ayahuasca. Ceremony begins when you sign up for a retreat and lasts for weeks after you drink the brew. It is a commitment of several weeks. The point of ceremony is to have a transformational experience, which requires sacrifice and preparation.

When our bodies are toxic, it becomes almost impossible for us to connect with these subtle energies. This is why we spend most days feeling numb to everything around us. While the vine helps us get closer to these energies, we must ensure we act as a clean vessel for them. There are instances where people go through extreme purging before participating in these sessions. For example, in Peru, some ceremonies begin with a *huancawi* purge, where a tonic made by the huancawi plant is consumed. The aim is to ensure you are as receptive as possible to these energies before you begin.

What happens if you ignore these guidelines? Most probably, you will be spending a better part of the ceremony itself cleansing your energies. This could mean feelings of nausea, discomfort, diarrhea, and vomiting during sessions. If you come prepared, you will likely find connecting to these sacred energies much more accessible. Above all, following the *dieta* shows a deep reverence and respect for the spirit of ayahuasca, and she will respond in kind when the two of you meet in the ceremony room.

These *dietas* are supposed to have a few benefits for all participants:

- **They help the body in healing itself**. Whatever we put our bodies through profoundly impacts our overall health and spiritual disposition. During this period of abstinence, our body begins to listen to its signals (which might have been lost). It learns to take care of itself and treat itself like a pure and sacred thing.

- **Not only do they help in preparing for these experiences, but they also help us recover quickly after the ceremonies**. Since these sessions leave us emotionally, mentally, and physically vulnerable to many energies (good and bad), we need protection to help us reintegrate safely. Dietas can help us do that.

- **This is an excellent first step if you're taking part in this ceremony to start making changes in your own life**. After all, as difficult as it might seem in the beginning, these preparations inculcate a sense of discipline in us. We learn to follow the rules for a higher purpose and might even stick to some of the changes we observe in our lifestyle. In any case, these *dietas* help purify our consciousness, which can help us become more spiritually inclined even beyond the ceremonies.

- **For those who seek an authentic experience, these *dietas* are not restrictions but assurances that we will have unique encounters**.

Another important reason we should follow the *dietas* mentioned here is that the Western diet and lifestyle are very different from the Indigenous one. Since the Indigenous people live in close communication with nature and mostly eat unprocessed food, their bodies and minds are already attuned to a plant-based life. On the other hand, the Western diet consists mostly of refined and processed food, an excessive intake of alcohol, and the presence of other preservatives and additives.

The same goes for the different kinds of drugs (both legal and illegal) that are taken regularly. Some of these medications are life-saving and necessary, but even they might have certain adverse effects when combined with psychoactive substances like ayahuasca. Many traditional guidelines wouldn't apply to us or would be too narrow in scope. Many Indigenous shamans might not even be aware of the potentially dangerous drugs that must be avoided before the ceremony. Therefore, we need to make considerations for them in our preparations.

There are three main areas of focus when it comes to a *dieta*: food and dietary choices, abstinence from stimulating substances and experiences and avoiding medical contraindications or side effects.

Dietary Guidelines

First, we will go over the foods that you need to avoid. While the guidelines differ slightly based on the retreat, there are a few common considerations. For one, you should avoid highly processed and refined foods as much as possible. This includes junk foods, foods and drinks that are extremely high in sugar, salt, and unhealthy fats, and even those that are incredibly spicy. Regarding meats, pork, and most red meat are supposed to be a no-no almost everywhere.

The best diet you can follow before this experience includes whole foods and is plant-based. Foods that occur naturally are the ones our body agrees with the most. Some of these foods, especially fruits and green leafy vegetables, will also help kickstart your metabolism (which could mean increased bowel movements). This effect will be compounded if you're not used to such a diet in your daily life. Don't worry; this is a good thing and an indication that your body has started its cleansing process.

Even otherwise healthy foods—like garlic, onions, different kinds of chilis, spices, foods high in citric acids, and fermented foods—are best avoided during this period. This is because, while eating clean and nutrient-dense foods is essential, it's equally important not to have foods that stimulate our senses.

According to shamanic teachings, spicy foods tend to have a *cutipado* effect on our senses. Roughly speaking, it means *bewitched*, which could affect the energies we're trying to channel through the vine. These foods are said to block or interfere with the channels we use to communicate with higher energies. In a more physical sense, these foods can cause unpleasant sensations if they come out during the ceremony. Think of this in terms of burning sensations, sickly feelings, and even an excessively sticky and sweet composition of the substances that come from us. We want any purging experience that does occur to be as pleasant (or the least unpleasant) as possible.

Tyramine and MAOIs

We should remember that the ayahuasca vine inhibits monoamine oxidase formation in our bodies, which is why we can experience its psychoactive properties. These MAOIs cannot process tyramine, which is naturally present in many foods. When tyramine is not broken down, it can lead to unpleasant sensations, including headaches, increased blood pressure, or nausea that does not lead to vomiting.

While these sensations are not harmful or threatening, they might lead to a suboptimal experience. This is why you should avoid food that contains tyramine, such as

- red meat

- aged cheeses like cheddar and parmesan

- pork

- peanuts (in excessive amounts)

- fermented foods like yogurt, kimchi, sauerkraut, fermented tofu, or soy sauce

- artificial sweeteners like aspartame

- alcohol

- chocolate (in excessive amounts)

- nutritional supplements such as protein powders

One thing to remember is that you might come across warnings regarding food interactions with MAOIs. While pharmaceutical MAOIs can cause extreme situations (including death) when taken with tyramine-rich products, this is not the case with ayahuasca. The effects of ayahuasca are reversible and short-lived, which is why there are no recorded fatalities from these interactions. However, it doesn't hurt to err on the side of caution.

When it comes to animal products in general, you should keep some things in mind. For one, most traditional ceremonies allow the consumption of chicken. However, these are usually free-range and locally found species. They are raised on farms or caught in the jungles. In contrast, most of the nonvegetarian food we consume comes from facilities where the animals aren't treated well, are kept in miserable conditions, and are pumped with different chemicals. Not only does this make them physically unhealthy for consumption, but it also makes them spiritually unfit.

When we talk about food or any form of consumption related to this ceremony, we want our energy to be as pure as possible. Thus, we're likely consuming the energy of an unhappy animal treated with cruelty. This is why it makes sense to be conscious about what you eat and where it comes from.

So, what should you be eating before the ceremony? You should eat whole, unprocessed grains, such as wild or brown rice, quinoa, and oatmeal. At the same time, you should eat fresh fruits and vegetables and legumes like green peas, lentils, and other pulses. You should avoid overripe fruits as well. In general, try to eat home-cooked vegetarian meals that use small amounts of oil (such as olive oil or coconut oil), salt, sugar, and spices.

Eat light, plant-based meals on the day of the ceremony. While you should drink adequate amounts of water or herbal teas, it's best not to observe a strict juice fast on or before the ceremony. For one, most juices are incredibly high in sugar and also eschew the benefits that come with the dietary fiber found in whole fruits and vegetables. Second, while eating light is recommended, not having solid foods can work against you.

An ayahuasca experience is a physically, emotionally, and mentally challenging experience. You might be in for one of your life's most energetically intense periods. Therefore, healthy foods will give you the energy to handle whatever comes your way later. Most people advise that your last meal should be taken at least four hours before the actual ceremony to give it time to digest. I usually stop eating around noon on the day of the ceremony, and I might have a little fruit in the early afternoon if I need more sustenance.

Avoiding Stimulation in All Forms

This part of your preparation focuses on spiritual cleansing in all forms. Traditionally, when shamans would go to the jungles, they would seek isolation to be alone with their thoughts and away from unnecessary distractions. Even in villages, which were usually close-knit communities, the days before the ritual would require people to stay inside their houses, minimize the number of interactions they had with others, and refrain from wasting their energy on idle gossip.

The modern world that we live in is stimulating in far more ways than before. On a normal day, we find ourselves inundated with numerous signals that try to engage our senses. If we want to watch something, we have a wide range of streaming services available. The same goes for choices in food, travel, and clothing. While we have more choices now, that doesn't necessarily mean we can make better decisions (or our lives are more fulfilling).

Most of us have to deal with *sensory overload*, which occurs when too much random information is thrown our way. Our brain gets so overwhelmed with all this that it tends to shut down. Our ancestors knew their flight-or-fight response would help them avoid danger and protect themselves and their families. For us, this has become a problem. When our bodies (and minds) are continuously stimulated, we cannot relax and may have problems functioning properly.

For example, if we're always stressed or in panic mode, we always feel tired. This works even when the stimulation makes us happy. If we're constantly chasing highs (through drugs, sex, or alcohol), our minds do not get a chance to allow our actual thoughts and feelings to meet us. We don't spend our time self-reflecting or understanding what we truly need. Most of these highs come from *wants* rather than *needs*.

Now, imagine if you were in this state before your ayahuasca experience. Chances are, you will neither have enough energy to participate fully nor act as the *blank slate* that these energies need to write (or rewrite) your narrative.

Avoiding Sexual Stimulation

Most cultures see sex as a powerful exchange of energy between two people. Whether in a long-term relationship or having casual sex with a stranger, a sexual encounter leaves a mark on each of you. Of course, some of these exchanges are more powerful than others, but all of them leave an impact on us. Now, when we're participating in an energetically intense ceremony, the energy of our recent sexual encounters will affect, and be affected by, these energies.

This might mean that you have experiences or visions that feature your sexual partners, or you might begin to feel more energetically linked with them than before. Not only can this be extremely overwhelming, but it might also confuse you. Whether we like it or not, we choose partners based on energetic reasons as much as physical and superficial ones. We might think we are making rational decisions, but often, we're responding to their aura. If their aura becomes too intense during the experience, we might get entangled (mentally, emotionally, or physically) with people who weren't meant to have such a profound effect on our lives.

Other than that, we might even find our energy reserves depleted when we need them during the ceremony. Some people believe that sex takes away from the energy needed for creative endeavors. Thus, it's recommended to abstain from sex or ejaculation for at least three days before the ceremony.

Avoiding Alcohol, Weed, and Caffeine

Alcohol, weed, and caffeine all are very strong stimulants. Hence, we should avoid them if we want an unadulterated experience. In some traditional societies, people are given a mix of marijuana, ayahuasca, or other plants. While there might be some reasons for this, and it might work in certain conditions, there is merit in consuming ayahuasca without the effect of anything else. I would avoid any teacher who uses this combination.

If nothing else, you would probably want to understand how this vine can help you in your journey ahead. If there are other psychoactive plants in the mix, you might not understand what is causing you to have this particular experience. Alcohol and caffeine cause havoc on your body when it is in the middle of a purge, and ayahuasca will not mix well with these substances. If you can't remove these stimulants during your *dieta*, I suggest you consider waiting for a moment when you have more control over your dependencies.

Another thing to keep in mind is the afterglow. Usually, an afterglow is the feeling of bliss or oneness with the world you enjoy after your psychedelic experience. We would understandably want to prolong this sensation for as long as possible. When we consume alcohol or other stimulants too close to the ceremony, we tend to experience a much shorter afterglow than we would like. I also recommend continuing your *dieta* for one week after your ceremony—ayahuasca will continue to work its magic if you leave your vessel clean after the ceremony.

At the very least, you should stop consuming alcohol and caffeine three days before the ceremony. However, it's advisable to do so two weeks before the session. If you are overly dependent on alcohol or your morning caffeine shot, the sooner you wean yourself off of it, the better. You'll likely have a few difficult days and face withdrawal symptoms; therefore, give your body enough time to recover before the ceremony. I remove alcohol and caffeine two weeks before the ceremony. This allows the body to recover properly from any withdrawals. During the week leading up to the ceremony, I fine-tune my body, remove food stimulants, and spend as much time alone as possible. Being alone is a fantastic way to prepare yourself leading up to the ceremony and can help you anchor yourself to Pachamama and the plant kingdom before meeting grandmother ayahuasca.

Digital Detox

A digital detox might be the hardest thing to do for most of us. We spend most of our days glued to our devices—television screens, laptops, or mobile phones. Admittedly, this will take more time than expected. However, minimizing our dependence on these before the ceremony is extremely important. Not only do they distract us, but they also affect our mental health.

While the blue light that is emanated from your screens has a negative effect on your sleep patterns, it can also cause your eyesight to weaken. Most importantly, the way we use our screens has a huge impact on our lives. Most of us spend a lot of time on social media. This gives rise to feelings of inadequacy, jealousy, and general discontent. Not only that, but we spend way too much time engaging with news that can upset us and make us feel hopeless.

Our devices provide an alternate world to escape, but this is sometimes a good thing. People who spend too much time online need help adjusting to the real world. Second, people immersed in the virtual world, or even in majorly practical concerns in the real world, usually have trouble sitting alone with their thoughts. When we partake in a mystical ceremony in such a state, there's a good chance that we won't get much out of it. We might become more frazzled when suddenly faced with these otherworldly energies.

How do you begin your digital detox? Start with things you're not overly attached to and go on to those that are tough to do away with. For example, you might find yourself sitting in front of the television for no reason other than being bored or distracted. Since there's nothing to look forward to, you can minimize your consumption relatively easily. Keep your phone away from you while sleeping; if you are working, try putting your phone on silent or removing it from your room.

You can minimize your use of digital screens before bedtime. Even if you stop using your phone or tablet one hour before sleeping, you will notice a significant shift in your mental and physical health. Blue light from screens influences your natural circadian rhythms. Taking a break from screens leads to better sleeping preparation. You can do this by replacing your current habit with a reading one. If you choose to read even 10 pages before bed (actual pages in a physical book), you will have less use for your phone. If you need help, you can always walk outside or talk to your family instead of staring at a phone before you sleep.

The last, but probably most difficult, aspect of this detox has to do with your social media engagement. If deleting your social media apps is too extreme, you can temporarily try deactivating your profile. If not, the least you can do is reduce the number of times you visit your profile or others. Resist the urge to interact with people or events virtually; instead, try to spend some time with yourself. This has benefits beyond the actual ceremony.

Most experts agree that people who consume less social media and are not addicted to their digital devices are usually happier and more content. For further reading on this subject, check out Cal Newport's book *Digital Minimalism: Choosing A Focused Life In A Noisy World,* which offers some great research and advice on reducing digital behavior in our lives. His main premise is that we should be more mindful and intentional when engaging with technology.

Avoiding Contraindications

This is the most crucial guideline for anyone on any kind of medication. Contraindications refer to certain conditions where it's advisable not to take a particular medicine or treatment. In other words, while these medications are valuable and necessary for you, they will potentially cause harm when taken alongside ayahuasca.

Even if you use other substances or supplements, you should pay special attention to this list. This is because most supplements are not regulated with the same rigor as drugs and medicines.

The most important thing here is that even well-intentioned shamans might not know the medications you're on and cannot give qualified advice on what to avoid and why.

The other thing is that many of these medications need regularity when you are on prescription. Most medicines can be avoided for some time, but some cannot. Therefore, one of the first things to consider is whether you can temporarily stop your medication. While many retreats are becoming more alert to these conditions, the responsibility primarily lies with you. Here are some of the major concerns around medications:

- **Selective serotonin reuptake inhibitors (SSRIs)**: Most antidepressants are SSRIs, and any mood enhancers or migraine medications that affect our serotonin levels can have an adverse effect on us when taken in combination with ayahuasca. Specifically, there is a risk of serotonin syndrome that is extremely dangerous. When two or more drugs interact, there is an increase in the serotonin levels in our bodies. When serotonin levels are normal, it helps properly function our brains and nerve cells. This is why it directly impacts our moods and sleep cycles. However, too much of it can cause a wide range of symptoms, from relatively mild ones like shivering, headache, diarrhea, insomnia, and elevated blood pressure, to severe ones like high fever, tremors, seizures, unconsciousness, and an irregular heartbeat. In some extreme cases, it can also cause death. You have a chance of contracting this syndrome when you increase the dosage of your regular drugs or combine one with another (as in this case). This is why most retreats ask you to stop taking these medicines as much as six weeks in advance. However, you also need to consider if that is possible. Never alter your dosage without consulting your doctor, and follow their advice if they believe you should not stop taking these medications, even for a short period.

- **MAOIs**: Pharmaceutical MAOIs can harm our health if taken in conjunction with ayahuasca, which is already an inhibitor. Some of how this reaction could affect us include cardiovascular diseases, extreme hypertension, cerebrovascular diseases, frequent headaches, and severe liver and kidney impairment cases.

- **Plant-based and other decoctions**: As discussed earlier, there are many reasons to avoid mixing different plant-based decoctions or other natural mixtures without supervision or in a careless manner. While some of these might not cause any harmful effects, some need to come with warnings. For example, there is a practice of smoking the secretions of Bufo alvarius (commonly known as the Sonoran Desert toad) along with ayahuasca. While some might believe this causes more intense experiences, it comes at a significant cost. Two compounds—bufotenin and 5-MeO-DMT—react adversely with the harmaline found in ayahuasca. There have been rare instances where this has caused death. Therefore, you should wait a few days after taking ayahuasca if you want to smoke this decoction. Another plant that one needs to be careful about is the toé, also known as Brugmansia or angel's trumpet. Some shamans are used to preparing the ayahuasca brews with toé. When the dosage is too much, it can lead to death. Even in cases where it's used for a long time, it can cause permanent mental impairment. This is why it's advisable always to ask what goes into your brew, and if you're not comfortable with something, don't try it.

- **Herbal supplements**: A few popular herbal supplements block ayahuasca in potentially dangerous ways. These include kava, kratom, St. John's Wort, and Ginkgo biloba. Again, many people might not be aware of how these supplements affect us when we take ayahuasca, so it's best to avoid taking them for a specified period before the ceremony.

While common sense indicates that we don't take any other psychedelics such as MDMA, psilocybin, or LSD during this time, it's also helpful to check if any other medication you're on can have an adverse effect during the ceremony. Also, this is important: *if you can't discontinue the medication you're taking currently, please postpone having your ayahuasca experience until things change.*

I completely understand the eagerness to try something that helps you deal with long-standing issues. In some cases, these include depression or chronic pain. However, the risks associated are high enough for you to consider everything before making this decision. If you have any doubts, please speak with the ayahuasca teacher or retreat facilitator well before the ceremony.

Social Preparation

We've discussed earlier that a *dieta* doesn't only prepare us physically but also psychologically. Our social lives result from our interactions with people and their energies. As hard as we might try, it's difficult to keep ourselves detached from these energies. While there are many benefits of social interaction, there are enough things to be concerned about. For example, if we belong to a toxic workplace, we might be regularly affected by the politics and negative vibes surrounding us. Similarly, those energies might also affect us if we know someone prone to gossiping about others.

According to ancient shamanic beliefs, we're never truly alone. We have many guides, angels, and spirits around us. We're not always fully aware of these energies (even if we can sometimes sense them). These energies also affect our ties with the people around us (and even those no longer with us).

Some of these energies are there to protect us, while others might be more toxic. Some of these might feed off of our energy, depleting us in the process. While our physical relations affect our mental and emotional health, these relationships affect us energetically. The veil between the material and spiritual worlds becomes thinner during the ayahuasca ceremony. This means we are prone to absorbing these energies, which might enter our systems and create havoc.

This is why isolation has always been a shaman's best friend before the ceremony. If possible, you should try to take some time off work before and after your session. During this time, you should get in touch with yourself. Even if it's impossible to cut yourself off from the world completely, you can minimize exposure to negative people and scenarios. If you find it impossible to detach from the negativity in your life, the least you can do is foster more positivity inside you. This will be challenging if you're in a difficult situation each day, but meditation, positive affirmations, and gratitude journaling can help you feel better.

Psychological Preparation

While different people have different experiences in ayahuasca ceremonies, most of us would agree that it is nothing like anything we've experienced before. This is why we prepare ourselves emotionally and psychologically for the journey. By preparation, I don't mean having specific expectations of the process. While we should have a general sense of *why* we're going through the process, we shouldn't be too keen on directing the *how* part of it. We'll discuss this more in our section on intention setting.

We must ensure that our minds are ready to go through this experience. There are some things we can do to prepare.

Gaining Awareness Through Self-Reflection and Journaling

If you want a therapeutic experience through ayahuasca, it helps to gain some perspective on your life before going in. If any traumatic experiences have shaped you or any incidents that have affected you deeply, chances are you've repressed those memories deep within you. This is a common defense mechanism employed by our ego so that we can continue to function in the world. However, during an ayahuasca experience, there's a good chance that these walls will come crashing down.

Therefore, it's a good idea to start becoming more aware of yourself in the present. This would include taking into account your past. What we are today heavily dependent on who we were yesterday. Self-reflection is not an easy journey. One thing you can do is start writing in a journal. This doesn't have to be an elaborate affair; all you need to do is start taking notes on anything that stands out during your day. For example, someday, you might find yourself in an unusually bad mood and not understand what is causing it. Or, you might notice that your energy levels get depleted when you think of something or visit a particular place. If you are prone to anxiety attacks, you might be unaware of some repetitive triggers in your life.

When we journal, we find a way to structure our usually chaotic thoughts and feelings on a blank page. This simple act is intensely powerful in many ways. We see patterns emerge when we regularly note down our thoughts and reactions. Writing is powerful not only because it can help us give voice to our ideas but also because it can help give birth to new ones. You might find different approaches that work for you or begin understanding the impact a particular incident has had on you.

A journal makes you feel less lonely on this path. As I said earlier, self-reflection is a challenging process, and most of us want to avoid doing the work for as long as we can. This means that you might find yourself alone on this journey, especially if your friends or family are going through a different phase of their lives. If you have a therapist, you can engage with them on these issues. You can ask for help becoming more self-aware (which should already be a part of your therapy) and look for more tools to help you get there.

Even if you aren't already in therapy, you might still find *talking* to your journal extremely calming. If you have a friend or family member with whom you can talk about your experiences, behavior patterns, or other issues, try to start a conversation with them. You don't need to mention your intentions of taking ayahuasca unless you trust them completely, but you can still ask them for guidance on this journey within yourself.

While you do this, keeping your judgment out of it is essential. You might feel tempted to feel guilt, shame, or anger at yourself. This isn't a means to amplify your self-loathing tendencies but rather an opportunity to give yourself the kindness and grace needed to do challenging inner work.

Gratitude while journaling is a great place to start—what are three things you are grateful for today? Next, you might review your day yesterday, look for something positive, and write down what it was and how it made you feel. Next, consider what you did that you felt you could have done better and jot down a few ideas for how you might have behaved differently. Keeping things simple is the best way to journal—sometimes, I'll just put the date, draw something like a happy face, and write a few keywords of gratitude. All gratitude is deposited in a universal vault of goodness that elevates humanity. You will find that contributing to that vault in your life will also elevate you.

Keeping a Dream Journal

Most of our deep-seated issues and traumas are rooted in the subconscious. A popular term that most healers and therapists now use is the "inner child." People think of this as a separate entity—a part of our subconscious—that records all our deepest childhood fears and aspirations. This inner child has undergone many trials and tribulations and is generally ignored by the adult version of ourselves. This, too, is an act of protection.

However, there are certain times when the inner child is active. A spiritual journey is one of them. If you're undergoing a spiritual awakening, you will likely meet your inner child along the path. They will guide you toward the wounds you need to heal and the opportunities for joy and love that await you. A child, after all, is both innocent and wise. They believe in the goodness of people and the limitlessness of possibilities, but they're also attuned to energies we've closed ourselves off from. This is why our inner child usually carries a lot of trauma, and spending time on healing this inner child will bring us closer to the life we're meant to live.

The other time when your subconscious becomes active is when you sleep. During this time, your subconscious mind tries to communicate with you through dreams. Admittedly, we forget most of them when we wake up, and not all are significant to us. However, there is enough material there to help us understand ourselves better.

Some people try to practice lucid dreaming, in which they become aware that they're dreaming. In other words, they're still in a dream state and conscious of their dreams. This is extremely helpful when we have trouble remembering our dreams (as most of us do) and when we want to get ideas about ourselves through our subconscious mind. Think of it as a psychedelic-free mind-bending experience.

While lucid dreaming is powerful, there are a few things to remember. This isn't an accessible state and takes a lot of time and practice. You probably cannot access this state within a few days or weeks. Two, since this experience works on blurring the lines between your dream state and awake mind, it can cause complications for those who already suffer from mental health issues.

It's also an elaborate practice we won't discuss in this book. However, what we can do is borrow an element from it. Usually, the first step most teachers recommend when initiating someone into a lucid dreaming practice is keeping a dream journal. In this journal, you begin to note down any dreams or fragments you might remember after waking up. Initially, you might not have much to go on. Slowly, however, your mind will be conditioned to allow you to make more elaborate notes. These notes might give you some idea of the issues you want to address during the ceremony.

Spending Time in Nature

How we live in this world regularly keeps us disconnected from nature. Even though everything we have—all that is essential and life-affirming—is a gift of nature, most of us have forgotten this sacred relationship. Most of us have become exploitative in our behavior toward nature. We can already see the effect of this on our environment and our lives. This disconnect can seem even more intense when we enter into a relationship with one of the most scared plants we know.

Ayahuasca is one of the giant pillars of plant medicine and is the *mother of all medicines* in the rainforest. Many people like to associate this plant with Divine Feminine energy, giving it the respect it deserves. When we think of Mother Nature, we know that we're in the presence of a nurturing, intelligent, and intuitive force. It's also incredibly playful and joyful, so we get a serotonin and oxytocin boost when we spend time with it. One of the reasons that the knowledge of this brew has been a closely guarded secret for a long time is that the *ayahuasqueros* believe that you need to be worthy of the vine. This includes people who work with the vine and those who receive its grace. That is why people say you might experience a calling when it's time to enter into communion with Mother Ayahuasca.

Even if you weren't going to an ayahuasca ceremony, spending more time in nature has far too many benefits for you to resist. You can build this relationship slowly and leisurely. If you're not used to spending time outdoors, you can try to spend some time walking on grass, especially in the morning. This small act can help reset your mind and give you a sense of positivity going forward with your day. If you're lucky enough to have a park or nature trail close by, take advantage of it and try to visit it as regularly as possible. My choice is to commune with the ocean. I am so grateful to have a deep relationship with the magical properties of water. I encourage you to explore long walks along the waterways and dips into the water if you live near a body of water.

You can also attune your senses to the different sounds and sights that nature bestows on you. How many of you have used an app that simulates or captures sounds of nature, usually in the form of gently falling rain, ocean waves, or birds chirping in trees? Why not give the real thing a try? While these sounds are less predictable, that is where their true beauty lies. Another thing that you can do is use your sense of touch and smell when in nature. You should exercise some caution here, especially because not every plant is made for touch and can be toxic or harmful in other ways.

That being said, you can always gently touch the bark of a tree or feel its leaves rustle against your fingers. These might seem romantic behaviors, but you are about to embark on a tryst with a powerful plant. Why not open yourself up to the many blessings it might bring?

Yoga and Mindful Movement

Indeed, the ayahuasca experience is primarily mental and spiritual; however, the body is certainly a considerable part of it. We began by understanding how different foods affect our physical and mental health during the ceremony. The same goes for exercise. If you're already physically active, try sticking to the routine as much as possible. Building your physical endurance might help you during and after this intense ceremony.

Yoga is an ancient Hindu and Buddhist practice that can be beneficial in this regard. For one, yoga is not just a physical exercise. It draws strength from a deep understanding of the human body, mind, and spirit. Only when we understand how different energies impact our bodies can we truly appreciate the power of yoga. In many cultures, yoga, and meditation go hand in hand, which should give you a clue about the interconnectedness between the two. It's also believed that in ancient Hindu societies, people training to be master meditators (those who meditated for long periods and accessed different metaphysical planes through the practice) also learned yoga. This gave them the physical strength and endurance needed to practice for long hours.

The other thing that yoga helps with is discipline. Since the practice can be rigorous and precise, it helps us become more focused. This focus can help us even after the ceremony when we need to recreate our lives. Remember that this journey is meant to start a new, hopefully lifelong, one. Any relationships you form with yourself during this time will stay with you for the foreseeable future.

If you aren't a vast exercise fan, try incorporating other forms of mindful movement into your schedule. If you're spending more time in nature, you should already be spending some time walking during the day. If you enjoy dancing (irrespective of whether you're good at it), dedicate some time to it each day. If nothing comes to mind, spend some time playing with friends or family. This burst of energy will serve you well during the ceremony.

Setting Intentions for Your Ceremony

Remember when we spoke about managing expectations regarding the ceremony? The thing is, you're participating in this ceremony for a reason. Even if you don't know exactly what you're looking for, you will usually sense that you want more from your life. While it's impossible to predict how a ceremony will go or where it will take you, you should try to get an idea of what you want from the session.

This is where intention setting comes into play. Most of us seek a spiritual or therapeutic experience from the ceremony. However, this needs to be narrower for you to get actual results. If you want to start creating a new life for yourself, you need to know what elements of your life you want to change, what areas you want to grow in, and what keeps you from achieving the life you want.

Your intentions are like signals to your subconscious mind telling you to get ready for whatever you want. All the time you spend in self-reflection—understanding yourself better and getting to know your strengths and weaknesses—will eventually help you set your intentions for the ceremony. You can also use your journal for this. Note down the areas of your life you feel satisfied with, but also acknowledge where you would like to see more growth. Maybe there's a talent you have, but you are unsure whether you should pursue a career based on it. Maybe you enjoy doing something but aren't sure if that is your life's purpose. Maybe you have experienced a few days or weeks of calm at a new place but don't know if this is the right time to make a long-term move.

We hold ourselves back from so much in our lives that we miss the good things right before us. Why not set an intention that helps you realize your blessings and live a happier life? Why not ask the spirits to show you where your true path lies?

The same goes for negative experiences or traumas. If you have anger issues, spend some time thinking about where they arise from. If you cannot trust people easily, can you remember instances where you chose to and were betrayed? Are there any difficult emotions that you've been holding on to forever? This doesn't pertain simply to emotional or mental things. You might want to heal your relationship with money. Or, you might want to experience less fear when you try new things. Ask yourself how you usually move through this world. Is there something you would like to change?

Our relationships are a massive part of our lives. They affect us deeply, and most decisions are based on them. Before participating in the ceremony, take some time to analyze your relationships. This could be your past relationships or your current ones. You might think that, with past relationships, you don't have much control. However, our past relationships can often cause us a lot of pain. We might even have certain traits we've developed only because of our past experiences. In these situations, the best intention you can set is to forgive others for the pain they've caused you. At the same time, you might want to take accountability for how you've failed to show up for others. Our lives and current relationships will dramatically improve if we *let go*.

When we look at our present relationships with people, we can invite them to discuss their issues with us. Even if we have good relations with those we care about, there's always space for improvement. Most of the time, we have blind spots regarding our roles in our connections with others. Letting others tell us what we need to work on can be very helpful. After this, you can set intentions that help you improve your relationships, form deeper connections, and move confidently through the world.

It's important to remember that not everything about us has to change. There are things we want to keep intact, qualities that this world has no value for. What if you're struggling to remain optimistic in the face of recent events? What if you've been naturally trusting, but a bitter experience has left you paranoid? What if you want to feel less jaded about things that used to excite you? What if you know exactly what you want but cannot take the first step?

As you can see, these intentions are unique to you and can only be formed once you have clarity about yourself. This is where I will also talk about having extremely specific expectations for the session. If you go into the ceremony saying things like, "Tell me how to make more money" or "Show me the exact method of starting my venture," you will likely be disappointed. It's like chaining a free spirit and asking them to dance to your tunes.

Once you know what you want to focus on, the next step is to let yourself go. I'm not saying that you won't receive answers or helpful insights; all I'm saying is that you don't get to decide how those answers come to you or what they look like. This is something to remember whenever you're involved in a spiritual experience. Whether we deal with tarot, astrology, or any rituals that deal with divination (predicting the future), we tend to demand exact answers. The truth is Spirit does not always communicate with us directly. We need to give it space to express itself.

Emotional Support

Some of us might feel worried about going through such an intense experience alone. While these ceremonies are usually held in groups, it might help to have a few familiar faces to go through the sessions with. This is also why some people conduct these ceremonies in intimate settings, such as their homes. However, it's still essential to have a trained guide with you.

You can attend the first few ceremonies with trusted friends and family members. Make sure that these people are willing to go, understand the situation and environment well, and trust you in the same way. This will give you the confidence needed to go through with the ceremony. However, be careful not to use these friendships as crutches that might prevent you from doing the hard work. Sometimes, having a friend along can distract us from full expression, and in other moments, they can act as support when we need it. Like most things, this delicate dance requires an open heart, honesty, and mindfulness.

Now that we're prepared for the ceremony let's see how the first night of ayahuasca unfolds.

Three

The First Night

My recommendation, particularly to those who are having feelings of ambivalence and concern from the very beginning, is to drink the medicine with a big "Yes" in their hearts and minds.

~ *Ayahuasca*, Javier Regueiro

The first night of taking the sacred vine can be overwhelming in more ways than one. The effects of ayahuasca can show up in the participant in as little as 10 minutes. Sometimes, it can take longer, but usually, things begin to change after the first hour. As mentioned, different shamans use different plants in conjunction with ayahuasca, and each has its formulae. This means that— depending on who administers the brew—the time in which the effects appear and the intensity of these effects will vary.

The same goes for your state of mind (remember set and setting). How the brew affects you will depend greatly on how you feel before and during the process. While some retreats can create strong brews, others believe lighter brews can do the trick. The facilitator will ask you how much ayahuasca you want when you are being served— let your intuition be your guide. It's easy to get wrapped up in your ego when others ask for larger doses or go back for additional cups. Stay true to your inner voice and ask for what is right.

The Experience

Every ayahuasca experience is different. Some people receive lots of visions, and some participants receive none. Spirits could visit you, or you might see people shapeshift into animals or other people. You could have a visit from an ancestor or even a dead relative. Some people purge nonstop, and others never purge at all. There is no way to shape our ceremonial journeys other than to prepare well with a solid *dieta* and focus on some of the things we discussed in chapter two.

In this book, we won't go into different experiences people have had with ayahuasca, though I will share some of my adventures where appropriate. The Recommended Reading section at the end of this book lists several beautiful resources for further exploration of the ayahuasca experience.

Many of these experiences, when described, can sound eerily similar. There can be two reasons for this. One is that Spirit might have some preferred modes of manifesting itself before us. There may be colors, visions, or sounds that convey an all-important message to anyone who drinks the brew. Another reason is that a lot of what we expect in the ceremony might be affected by what we've already read in the different accounts of others. While it's always helpful to know how these experiences have changed people or helped them, the images can affect us much deeper than expected. The best state of mind when approaching the ayahuasca experience is to release all forms of expectation. Remember that ayahuasca gives you what you need, not what you want.

Let's focus on the nature of these experiences and try to understand what we can do to make the best of the journey. One of the most recognizable effects of taking any psychedelic is the ability to see visions. These visions can be abstract or precise. Usually, people report seeing different colors, sounds, or lights. Your mood at the time can play a role in how these visions appear before you. If you don't have a vision, don't worry about it. It's common for people participating in the ceremony for the first time not to have any visions. Some shamans even believe that it might take some time for the spirit of the vine to get acquainted with that of the participant. If you have a mystical experience, it will likely be as difficult to refute as it is to describe.

What's far more common in these ceremonies is that you will come face-to-face with your true nature. Sometimes, the spirits within us are the scariest to confront. During this session, you might suddenly remember long-forgotten memories. These might be delightful, but the memories we repress are usually not the kindest ones. The same goes for emotions. You might feel things much more intensely than you ever have before. Even incidents or experiences that you might have dealt with lightly in the past could bring up reactions that make no sense to you. You will feel more vulnerable during this time than you want, but you won't seem to have a choice.

In some rare cases, there might be feelings of paranoia as well. When we feel paranoid, we might respond to deep-seated fears in an irrational manner. An episode of paranoia can present itself like mental illness in clinical conditions. However, they're usually expected in the context of an ayahuasca experience. Moreover, these episodes are generally over quickly.

While an average ayahuasca experience can last between four to six hours, the problematic periods—including feelings of disorientation or helplessness—usually last for no more than half an hour. This also depends on the intensity of the brew itself, as well as on other factors such as the set and setting and whether you've taken more than one round of the drink. Again, these are less common in sessions for beginners, but you should keep them in mind.

Let's now discuss what you can do to have an optimal experience.

Pay Attention to Your Body Language

A ceremony is a dance of trust. Not only are you trusting your facilitator and, to some extent, your co-participants, but you're also trusting the unknown. You want to get closer to the unknown, which cannot happen until you learn to surrender to the journey. Whether you observe mystical phenomena or a different version of yourself, you must allow these things to happen. As Tony Robbins said when I went to his Unleash the Power Within event, "Life is happening for you and not to you." Realize that what happens in the ceremony is for your growth. Ayahuasca is a wise and gentle spirit, but she might need to turn up the discomfort to help you learn a lesson or two.

Trusting is also about being open to receiving from spirit. Our first line of defense or receptivity is found in our body language. Think of it this way: When we approach someone with balled-up fists or listen to someone with our arms crossed, we give them the impression that they're not welcome or appreciated. Sometimes, this is deliberate, but other times, we're simply giving off the wrong signals without being aware of it. These subtle gestures can have a profound impact on our relationship with spirit. So much of how we feel about others is related to the vibes that emanate toward them with our energy.

If people can pick up on energies, it's hard to believe that spirits cannot. We might not want to appear closed off or scared, but our bodies could convey that message. How do we take care of this? Let's go back to the previous example. When you need to convey warmth or friendship, you are asked to have more *open* body language. This will include facing toward the other person, making sure your posture is relaxed, and talking to them in a receptive manner. This is what you need to do as well. Be as relaxed as possible, and make sure you welcome the experience.

Welcome the experience with mindfulness and openness—treat grandmother ayahuasca as if she were a dear friend or family member. I recommend sitting up straight and extending your spine to receive the universe's energies. Let those cosmic energies flow through you and into grandmother. The journey you're about to embark on is similar to life's journey. You might find yourself happy (or euphoric) one moment and sad the next. Similarly, you might have a moment of epiphany followed by stretches where you feel bored and underwhelmed. Be ready to experience it all—the beauty, the terror, the joy, and the pain.

When you're facing periods when nothing seems to happen, stay present. Physically, this would mean that you stay within the ceremony space until it's deemed safe for you to leave. Most people don't recommend driving or even walking on your own in such a condition. This is because the effects of the drug don't follow a pattern. You might feel like nothing's happening and experience something intense after some time has passed. In any case, your facilitators know best, so always listen to them no matter what. And, if you feel that something's wrong, reach out to your guides without hesitation.

It's also possible for you to mentally check out. This is also not recommended because your mental state will affect the work of the medicinal plant. Therefore, it's important to stay engaged during periods of lull. If you are having difficulty staying present, try and anchor yourself to the music or an image in the room.

Ego dissolution is a common experience in the ayahuasca journey, and let me tell you that it feels great, but it can also bring up fear as our identity slips away. I had one journey where I merged with God and disappeared into the divine. My ego surfaced and reminded me that I had a body and responsibilities to return to. The ego reminds us of who we are and what we like and don't like. It also directs our lives.

What happens when this ego dissolves into nothingness? In one sense, we cease to exist. Our ego places us firmly on this plane of existence, and as it dissolves, we begin to exist in everything. We feel connected to everything, become a part of divine consciousness, and see everything as an interconnected web—it is here where we step into oneness and drop the separation created by the ego. Ayahuasca assists this delicate dance and opens a door toward the divine.

This experience, which can be scary and exhilarating at different times, can make the best of us feel unmoored.

What do we do then? Do we shrink away from the experience, or do we lean in? I know it's easier said than done, but we'll discuss ways to keep ourselves steady during the challenging parts of the experience.

Let's go back to the body language analogy. It's generally believed that people who maintain eye contact during conversations are deemed trustworthy. Think of this experience as maintaining steady eye contact with your deepest self and not flinching when you most want to. When the spirit of ayahuasca looks into your soul, open your body, mind, and heart to her majesty.

Taming the Monkey Mind

According to Buddhist teachings, the *monkey mind* is the part of us that does what it wants. Much like a petulant and trying child, this part of our brains is whimsical and unreliable. It's also extremely restless and indecisive. When it wants to do something, it doesn't ask for permission. Most of us find it impossible to control this monkey mind of ours—however, developing a practice that helps us rein in the monkey mind is essential for a good life. The Buddha reminds us of the power of getting a handle on the monkey mind: "The mind is everything. What you think, you become."

Our ego is primarily concerned with protecting and caring for itself, right? Well, the monkey mind is also thought to be part of our ego. This is not surprising after seeing how self-serving it can be. While there are aspects of our ego that protect us, there are many others that keep us from realizing our true potential. Our monkey mind can be extremely noisy, and most of that chatter is unsuitable for us. For example, we might want to do something that makes us happy, but our monkey mind tells us we're not good enough. We might want to take a chance on someone, but our monkey mind talks us into fear and away from courage.

The monkey mind holds us back by creating self-doubt and sabotaging our confidence. When we want to get something done and cannot, it's usually our monkey mind to blame. It distracts us—often with fears, worries, and sometimes whimsical notions that keep us from achieving what we want.

We know our monkey mind is wild, but can we tame it? If so, how? It turns out that the answer lies with the Buddhists themselves, and it's known as mindfulness.

Mindfulness

Mindfulness is a mental state achieved by focusing one's awareness on the present moment while calmly acknowledging and accepting one's feelings, thoughts, and bodily sensations. The philosopher Jiddu Krishnamurti described mindfulness as choiceless awareness. He said, "In awareness, there is no becoming, no end to be gained. From which understanding comes, there is silent observation without choice and condemnation."

Mindfulness is about paying attention in a particular way: on purpose, in the present moment, and non-judgmentally. This involves being aware of one's thoughts and feelings as they occur, without reacting to them or becoming attached to them. In awareness, there is full acceptance of what is without the desire to change the present into something else.

By practicing mindfulness, we can learn to be more present in our daily lives, be more aware of our surroundings, thoughts, and feelings, and manage our emotions better. Research has shown that mindfulness can have several benefits, including reducing stress, improving focus and concentration, and promoting feelings of well-being.

Mindfulness encourages us to focus entirely on whatever occupies us at the moment—and when unwelcome thoughts come, we accept them without any judgment. Do you begin to see the link between this practice and our ayahuasca experience? When we have unpleasant feelings or sensations, our first instinct is to brush them away or do everything we can to avoid them. This way, we close ourselves off from the lessons found in challenging moments.

When we begin to practice mindfulness, we become more grounded during unsettling experiences. Instead, we feel a sense of calm and acceptance that helps us understand the true meaning behind the experience. When we're in a mindful state of being, we begin to let go of our expectations from the present moment. We don't tell ourselves how to act or feel; instead, we're content to *simply be* and let the experience unfold.

An ayahuasca experience can provide moments of extreme calm, and in those moments, we feel like nothing else matters. These moments are very close to the way we feel when we become genuinely mindful in our lives. Our monkey mind dissolves entirely during this experience. However, we usually react to this with resistance. We feel out of control because this is all we've ever known. So, when the chatter dies down, do we want silence? In the beginning, the answer is no. This is where daily mindfulness practice can help us.

There are many ways in which you can practice mindfulness:

- **Try mindful eating**: You should begin with an activity you do every day. Most of us have gotten into the habit of eating distractedly. We barely engage with our families during lunch or dinner, preferring to watch TV or stare into our mobiles during the meal. One of the simplest exercises one can do is called the raisin exercise. You don't have to use a raisin; you can choose whatever food you want. The important thing is to engage all your senses while eating and to be mindful of the food before you. According to this exercise, we should observe the food before eating it. We should inspect it carefully if it's something we can hold, such as a raisin or a piece of corn. We should take in its scent, color, and texture. After that, we can slowly begin eating it, taking in all its flavors. This way, the food feels tastier and gives us more nutrients and energy. More importantly, we learn to stay present and engaged with the task. Eating is a very sensual experience, but we've stopped enjoying our food because of our hectic lifestyles. When we begin to eat mindfully, we bring back the joy of eating.

- **Mindful walking**: Since we've decided to spend more time in nature, we will learn to walk mindfully at one point or another. Again, the concept is deceptively simple. All we need to do is engage fully with the act of walking. This means no devices. If possible, this should include music that we hear through our earphones while walking or running. While music is an excellent accompaniment to these activities, it doesn't help with mindfulness. All we're doing at the moment is distracting ourselves with one more sound. Instead, we should try to immerse ourselves in the sounds of nature. Taking a deep breath in a forest or around trees can help reset our minds.

- **Visualization**: When our minds are extremely frazzled, we wish to escape into a kinder, softer world. The ideal world can be different for different people. For example, you might want to visualize spending time with your family on the beach. Consider spending time alone in the forest. You might wonder why we're using visualization for mindfulness. After all, the whole point is to immerse ourselves in the moment, right? The thing is, sometimes we need to make the present moment better. While visualization is not the same as being in a particular place, it has immense benefits. This is because our brains can be tricked into thinking that what we're visualizing is the experience. Not only does it help us breathe easier at the moment, but it also helps us set intentions for what we want our ideal life to look like. This isn't a byproduct of discontentment. It can help us manifest the kind of reality we want.

- **Mindful listening**: When it comes to our relationships, we can often be less engaged with our loved ones than we think. When it comes to work, this problem gets worse. Why is it important to listen? Traditionally, words have been given precedence over everything else regarding communication. The speaker must bear the burden of communication; they must speak clearly and fluently, engage the audience, and direct the discussion. The thing is, the audience doesn't need to listen, but they should. For one, so much communication is nonverbal. When deeply engaged with a speaker, we pick up on cues we might otherwise miss. Second, sometimes speakers have a lot of knowledge and insights to impart, but we are too distracted to listen to them. Speakers should be fluent and effective, but why can't we be graceful and attentive listeners? As mindful listeners, we give respect to those who are trying to communicate with us. Not only that, but we also provide them with valuable feedback regarding the information they provide us. This way, we create a real conversation between the speaker and us.

It will take time for you to get used to mindfulness—we are so used to living in the past and future that this paradigm shift requires practice. As you relax into mindfulness, you'll realize nothing is more important than this moment. When we learn to inhabit each moment fully, we'll have a more profound and less unsettling ayahuasca experience.

When our minds wander during an ayahuasca experience, we must bring it back to the present moment with ease. Mindfulness helps us immensely in this regard. The other things that can help us fully embrace this adventure are meditation and intention setting. We've already discussed intention setting in the last chapter, but we can now see its use during a troubling experience. When things become difficult, we need to remind ourselves why we're doing something in the first place.

Things will get difficult and intense during your ceremony. Remember to anchor your *why*. Why was it important for you to deal with your demons? Why was it important for you to show up to the ceremony? Why was it necessary to heal from your childhood trauma? When you remember your *why*, it is easier to move through challenges when the ceremony gets tough.

Let's now discuss meditation, specifically *mantra* meditation, in some detail. This is another powerful method of focusing on the experience without becoming overwhelmed.

Mantra Meditation

Meditation is the act of focusing our energy on a particular object, breath, or energy. This attention is not the same as obsessing over specific thoughts or feelings we may have. When we decide to focus on our energy, we gain insights about ourselves. This also helps us feel calmer and in control of our lives. This was an ancient practice in Hindu and Buddhist cultures. Meditation has immense physical, mental, and spiritual benefits for us, which is why it's gaining popularity among Western populations.

Meditation can help bring us back to the present when our mind wanders during the ayahuasca ceremony. It also keeps us from getting distracted in the first place. Our visions become clearer; we don't get tense during the ceremony and can integrate better afterward.

There are many different forms of meditation. Even mindfulness can be practiced as meditation. If you want to dive into guided meditation, I recommend the Waking Up app by Sam Harris. Sam is a neuroscientist with a deep interest in consciousness who explores concepts that help us uncover ways to live our best lives. He explores the theory behind meditation practice in his app by taking ancient wisdom and pressure-testing it with modern teachers, scientists, and scholars. Of course, you can't break out your phone during the ceremony and open his app for help, but he can help you prepare mindfully as part of your regular daily meditation practice.

Something you can take into the ceremony room with you is mantra meditation. What exactly is mantra meditation? The Sanskrit word mantra can be broken up into *man* (mind) and *tra* (transport). It's something that has the power to transport the mind. There's no widely accepted definition of what a mantra is. This is because mantras have deep spiritual significance for those who work with them. This concept originated in ancient Hindu and Buddhist traditions but has been spread across different religions and cultures.

According to this concept, words or utterances have power, and that power is carried through vibrations. When we utter anything, we're giving energy to it. Some of these words are higher in energy than others. For example, the *Om* sound is considered the Universe's vibration. We can also elevate our energies when we repeatedly utter these sacred words. When we say these mantras, we tap into a universal code that goes back thousands of years and resonates through sound vibration. These vibrations can help us reach higher states of consciousness and root us in the present moment during the ceremony.

Many experts believe that just as psychedelics are one way to have intense spiritual experiences, meditation is another. When we combine meditation with ayahuasca, we can increase the clarity and intensity of our experience.

Many people chant mantras as part of their religious worship. In these cases, it's important to chant specific mantras that pertain to the particular God being worshiped. For example, *Om namah shivay* (I worship Shiva) is a common Hindu phrase used by people to acknowledge Shiva as the Divine Masculine or Supreme Being. In Christianity, Ave Maria, Hail Mary, or Jesus might be used as a mantra. The same goes for Islam, Judaism, and other religions.

In some religions, there is no God to worship. For example, Buddhism is concerned with ideas of enlightenment and growth. According to its teachings, as long as we can look within ourselves and observe specific guidelines, we can achieve our true spiritual destiny. Here, *Om mani padme hum* (the jewel in the lotus) talks about the paths that lead to Divine Consciousness.

More complex mantras, especially in Hinduism, have very specific meanings. In some schools of Hinduism, these mantras are considered extremely sacred and powerful. It's also believed that the power within them lies dormant unless it's invoked through a special ritual by a teacher or spiritual guide.

This seems overwhelming for someone who has just been introduced to mantra meditation. However, many experts believe that a mantra is anything—a word, phrase, or thought—that gives you strength when needed. As long as it has special significance, you can create your mantra. It could be encouraging, saying, "I can do it." Or, it can help you instill confidence in who you are. For example, "I am a joyful being." Also, you don't need to chant these mantras out loud. As long as you can focus on the words uttered, you can also chant them in your mind. In some practices, it's believed that mantras that aren't uttered aloud are even more potent than those that someone can hear.

Some people become so adept at chanting these mantras that they don't need to think of them anymore consciously. The mantra will remain part of their awareness as long as they breathe. This is known as *ajapa* (*a–* standing for without and *–japa* standing for mantra or chant). Thus, this mantra is being chanted without a chant. Admittedly, this is not for beginners, but it's fascinating to think of these chants' potential.

Since mantra meditation can be a very effective way of controlling your monkey mind and might even bring you closer to the energies trying to communicate with you, you should try it. The first thing you need to do is choose the mantra. Start with something simple, like the powerful mantra "*Om.*" Find a comfortable place to relax or go for a walk in nature. Recite this mantra while seated with your spine straight, as it will help you focus on the practice. Once you're comfortable, start by inhaling deeply and then exhaling slowly.

Do this for some time until you can focus on your breath. After this, start chanting the mantra with each breath that you take. In the beginning, you can do this out loud to stay attentive. Later, you can chant it silently. If you obsess too much about the words, stop for some time and then start again. Remember, the entire process should be easy and free-flowing. When your thoughts wander, you should pause, acknowledge it, and then gently bring your mind back to the practice.

This will take some time, but soon, you will turn to these mantras automatically. When that happens, these sacred words become a part of your subconscious. That is when the real magic begins.

One of the other things to keep in mind is that your meditation practice doesn't have to be an elaborate ritual. While there are perks of committing half an hour or even 20 minutes each day to meditation, this might not be possible for beginners. The Waking Up app I mentioned earlier has a ten-minute mode where Sam walks you through the meditation—this is a great way to start your practice.

The good news is that you can start with as little as a few minutes of dedicated practice. You don't need a specific meditation space; you must be protective of the time you've set aside. While you can practice it any time of day—and some people like to meditate before going to bed—morning meditation is usually considered the best.

Consistency is more important than intensity as a beginner. If you miss out on a few days of meditation, don't worry about it. Try to meditate as regularly as possible, but don't use one missed day as an excuse to give up. With practice, you won't need any external motivation to meditate. While there are many rewards that meditation gives you, the process will act as its reward.

Breathing & Prana Exercises

You might oscillate between fear and trust during the ceremony as a beginner. This is to be expected. However, we must do everything to ground ourselves before and during the experience. One technique that helps immensely during moments of the challenge is breathwork. The relationship between breathwork and ayahuasca might be deeper than we think.

For one, we usually go through life breathing normally. However, when our fight-or-flight response is activated, this breathing becomes faster and shallower. Sometimes, we might even hold our breath for too long without realizing it. This indicates that we're not okay, and a vicious cycle is formed. One of the ways to relax ourselves during this time is deep breathing. When we consciously take longer and deeper breaths, our bodies get the signal that we are safe. Our stress hormone levels also go down.

Our breath is considered the secret to a longer life in ancient practices. It's believed that all of us come with a predetermined number of breaths. Thus, if we can prolong each breath's length, we will also prolong our lives. Also, it's believed that our breath is connected to our "life force," known as *prana* or *chi*. Therefore, by learning to control our breathing, we can control the energies that make up our lives and those connected to the Higher Consciousness.

This is why *pranayama*, which means to gain control of the life force, is used as a practice, often in conjunction with yoga, to control our breath in various ways for different lengths of time. In pranayama practice, there are four important aspects of breathing:

1) *Pooraka*, or inhalation
2) *Rechaka*, or exhalation
3) *Antar kumbhaka*, or internal breath retention
4) *Bahir kumbhaka*, or external breath retention

We know that breathing can help us ground ourselves in reality. What we don't realize is that it can also help us heal. In many ways, it works similarly to ayahuasca. Just as meditation can help us reach elevated states of consciousness, so, too, can breathwork. Many psychonauts have realized this connection. A leading example of this is Stanislav Grof, a psychiatrist at the forefront of the psychedelic revolution for decades. Interestingly, he has also developed and propagated a technique known as holotropic breathwork, in which different breathing techniques are used for emotional healing and reaching altered states of consciousness.

Many similarities emerge when we consider how breathwork functions compared to ayahuasca. For example, when we experience pain or trauma, we usually ignore or push them away. In one way, we're not completing the feedback loop that comes with a classic fight-or-flight response. Slowly, these tensions or negative energies get stored in our bodies and our consciousness. Then, they emerge later in the form of blockages in our bodies.

These blockages can be mental—like when we have fears or anxieties related to specific situations—or physical. These physical energy blockages can be the root cause of chronic pain. It's even believed that these energy blockages affect our bodies' chakras (energy centers), thus limiting us in different physical, emotional, and spiritual ways.

When we use ayahuasca for healing and personal growth, what happens is that these fears and traumas come to the surface. This can be unexpected and intense. Our first instinct is to summon our ego and protect ourselves. Sometimes, our ego does a thorough job of numbing us so that we might fall prey to various addictions. However, most defenses don't work when confronted with the sacred vine.

When we learn to work through these traumas by facing and acknowledging them in the beginning and then letting them go, we finally start getting rid of the blockages in our bodies. The most powerful thing we can do is let go of anything we've been holding on to for far too long. Ayahuasca helps us in this process, and so does breathwork.

Many people who have worked simultaneously with breathwork and ayahuasca believe that the two experiences have a mutually beneficial relationship. When we start participating in these ceremonies and working with the sacred vine, we become less resistant to trauma and healing work. This helps us with breathwork. At the same time, breathing consciously lets us delve deeper into healing with ayahuasca because we stop running away from ourselves. It's also believed that Divine Energy permeates both experiences, and it's not uncommon to find ourselves dealing with similar themes and visions during the two journeys.

Lastly, it's believed that our hearts are often constricted with fear and anxiety. When we learn to breathe deeply, our lungs expand, making more space for the heart to breathe (at a physical level) and opening up any energetic blockages in the heart chakra. Here, I would like to mention one common misconception about psychedelics. Most people think that taking psychedelics, including ayahuasca, is a self-serving act. While I can understand why people think it's indulgent, we become more connected to others than before when we take them in the right spirit.

For example, many people report that their ayahuasca journeys make them less judgmental, more empathetic, and more capable of experiencing unconditional love toward others. Of course, this helps them heal their traumas much faster, but its effects go far beyond that. This is why many people with profound experiences with psychedelics also become healers, teachers, and spiritual guides.

You will notice that the people around you will benefit from your ayahuasca journey. You are consuming ayahuasca for the entire world. Each cup you drink helps heal our collective consciousness and the traumas we carry as a society. You are healing yourself, your children, your partner, your ancestors, your siblings, your friends, your colleagues, your neighbors, and every other person you contact.

Deep Breathing

Now that we know how helpful breathing can be during and beyond ayahuasca let us learn some techniques that we can use.

Breathing is the simplest technique to center ourselves during a problematic ayahuasca experience. Here, we can inhale and exhale several times deeply without forcing our breaths. In the beginning, you can take three or five breaths in one set. Some people even like to belly breathe, as it helps to expand the diaphragm and lets more air into our bodies. This is said to be even more relaxing than breathing through our noses.

To practice belly or abdominal breathing, you must place your hand gently on your chest. Then, when you begin to inhale, ensure your chest does not rise (your hand should remain steady on the chest). Instead, inhale through your belly and watch your stomach rise and expand. When you exhale, purse your lips together to let your breath escape. Do this for sets of three in the beginning.

Once you get a simple rhythm down, extend your practice by inhaling for five seconds and extending your exhale for seven to ten seconds. Breathing through your nose on both the inhale and exhale, you want to make the exhale last longer than the inhale. Once you get this wired, hold your breath for a few seconds at the end of the inhale and exhale. In pranayama practice, breath retention is key to building your prana.

Some people also practice Anulom Vilom pranayama, an alternate breathing technique. Here, we sit cross-legged with our spines straight. Then, we place our thumb on the side of our nose to temporarily block the passage of air through that nostril. After that, we take a long and deep breath from the open nostril. After inhalation, we hold our breath for some time and use our middle and ring fingers to press the other side of the nose. The nostril that is now free is used for exhalation.

An important thing to remember with breathing techniques is that they can make you feel dizzy initially. Therefore, doing small sets is advisable until you grow more comfortable with them. Also, some exercises can be done while lying down, so try doing that when you're starting. For a deep dive into pranayama, grab a copy of *Asana Pranayama Mudra Bandha* by Swami Satyananda Saraswati.

Body Scan

The body scan technology is essential for using your breath to create awareness about your body and its issues. While you can do this technique at different times during the day to check in with yourself, this is especially helpful when you are feeling stressed or anxious. Remember how our bodies hold trauma, fear, and anger in different areas in the form of blocked energies? A body scan helps us identify those areas and then release the blockages.

You can do this technique while standing or sitting down. However, in the beginning, you can lie down so that you are fully relaxed and focused on the process. All you need to do is close your eyes and focus on breathing. Make sure you breathe slowly and consciously but do not use force. When your body gets used to the rhythm, bring awareness to each part of the body. You can start anywhere you like, but it's best to work sequentially, so you don't get confused.

You can begin at your toes and work up to the top of your head. When you inhale, focus on one part of your body. Bring your entire awareness to it and try to see how that area feels to you. As you breathe, you will notice if a particular area is in pain or feels tighter than usual. My tightness accumulates in my shoulders, abdomen, and jaw, where I usually start my body scan. You likely know your trigger points, so start in the known areas and move to the unknown. When you identify tightness, complete your breathing cycle while releasing anything causing this blockage. Breathe into the area of blockage through your nose and exhale the tension through your mouth. Veronica, one of my teachers, encourages visualizing breathing out through the tips of the toes, helping the body release in a powerful way. She suggests, "imagine colorful (be mindful of the specific color) fireworks shooting out of your toes."

Slowly, you will begin to get familiar with how your body responds to the trauma. Moreover, your body will also tell you if it's in a happy or relaxed state. These signals are useful when you have a particularly stressful episode. Even without realizing it, your stomach might store pain, or your chest might get tighter. When you realize this and use your breath to release the tension in these areas, you signal to your body to let go of the stress you're carrying.

This can be especially helpful during a challenging ayahuasca experience. It might take some time to get comfortable with this technique, but eventually, you will find yourself doing a quick body scan whenever things get uncomfortable. Both your body and your mind will thank you for it.

Anchors During a Difficult Experience

The techniques mentioned above can help you take care of yourself during an intense or challenging period in your ayahuasca journey. There are some other things you can do to navigate this experience smoothly.

For one, hold on to your intention—but hold it gently. Remind yourself as often as necessary about your reasons for going through this experience, and also invite in any lesson you might need beyond your intention.

Second, if there's music playing in the background, pay attention to it. Usually, when we're amid an experience, we can forget ourselves and get stuck in our minds. Music helps us reorient ourselves in the physical space by acting as an anchor. In shamanic ceremonies, music also acts as a guide. These pieces of music have deep spiritual significance to the shamans, and usually, they are attuned to the cosmic vibrations that we're trying to tap into. If nothing else, you will feel more relaxed as you concentrate on the songs.

Third, sit up straight and open your eyes. Sitting up straight will open your chakras and allow unobstructed energy to run through your kundalini system. Opening your eyes brings you into the present moment. When our eyes are closed, the visions can be rooted in our mental structures or fears. When we open our eyes, these visions are still a part of our awareness, but their intensity decreases considerably and tends to be rooted in the present moment. This is why it's advised that when you're witnessing something that seems too much to handle, you should remind yourself to open your eyes and sit up straight. Imagine your posture when you feel assertive and attentive—model that state of being as much as possible during your journey.

The Power of Gratitude

Last but not least, practice gratitude. This is something we can use even beyond the ceremony. Count your blessings each day and remain grateful to the universe. It's the human tendency to focus on things that are not going well or are missing from our lives. Even if we have enough to be thankful for, we will most likely look at someone else and want the things we don't have. This is even more pronounced in the age of social media. It seems like everyone other than us is having the time of their lives.

This is why starting a gratitude journal is recommended even before participating in the ceremony. This way, we'll get into the habit of noticing the numerous things that improve our lives. When we're amid our ayahuasca experience, we tend to run away from the dark parts. However, it's our shadow that gives us proof of the light.

A problematic experience can make us feel bitter or angry. No one wants to remember the unpleasant things we've experienced or the unpleasantness within us. However, if we practice gratitude during this time, our awareness shifts from darkness to light, from anger to love. When you practice this, be thankful for the difficulties as well. Challenges are unique opportunities to heal and often uncover parts of ourselves that we have hidden from the world. If you reach a painful moment in your journey, my teacher Natascha says to reflect on the fact that you are "love and light." However, please don't use it as a weapon or a shield. Relax into the intrinsic truth that you are love and light at your core.

How many people worldwide get a chance to work through their pain and trauma? How many of us have this experience where we can meet our true selves? How many can we reset our direction and control our destinies? This is not something you should take for granted. Once you realize that the whole ceremony— along with its highs and lows—is a gift, you will become more positive and humbler about the entire experience.

Rasha reminds us in her book *Oneness* that the hardest challenges can offer our deepest lessons and that our emotional release is the key to liberation from the patterns that keep us disconnected from our authenticity. She writes, "You must open your heart to the very real sensations of hurt, sorrow, or outrage... in so doing, you pave the way for the reintegration of a missing piece of your being."

Four

Preparation for Second Night

*If you intend to do plant medicine work, then consider
the integration to be an inseparable, nonnegotiable
part of the psychedelic journey,
and a time of self-care and self-love.*

~ Grandmother Ayahuasca, Christian Funder

Please sign up for a two-day retreat and commit to sitting
both nights, no matter what you feel after the first night.
I have watched people walk away after the first night, and
many never return to ayahuasca. It's essential that you
stay the second night and overcome any desire you might
have to run for the bleachers. At the beginning of my
relationship with ayahuasca, I wanted to run after the
first night many times, but I fought through my fears and
stayed every time. On the other side of that fight was a

ton of healing and beauty—I broke patterns I would have never overcome had I left the retreat before it was over.

Committing to both nights also gives you the space to retreat from all the hustle and bustle of your life. The ceremonial aspect of ayahuasca is a beautiful opportunity for you to disconnect from the outside world and reconnect with yourself. This is your time and your space to heal and rebuild. I recommend staying off your phone for the entire weekend—disconnect from anything that might distract you from going deep on your second night. Use this weekend to build a cocoon and let people know you'll reach out after the weekend. Set clear boundaries with yourself and others to create optimal conditions for a beautiful experience.

Let's get back to the first night—no matter how much you want to leave after the first night, I urge you to stay for the second. I keep saying this, but I want this idea to sink deep into your heart. My teacher Natascha says that the first night is the washer and the second is the dryer. The first night can often feel like your traumas and fears are being washed away, and the second night is for reflection and celebration—drying out what you washed away. It's not always like this, but the first night is often the hardest. Nonetheless, whatever happens during the first night, please stay for the second night—it's really important to commit to the entire weekend.

This experience brings with it a lot of conflicting thoughts and emotions. You might feel excited about having tried the brew for the first time. If you were exceptionally lucky, you might have had a mystical experience.

However, you might be unable to make sense of anything you've just experienced. You might even feel slightly disappointed if you had expected something dramatic to happen. Usually, people go into the experience wanting to feel everything in the first ceremony. They feel underwhelmed when this does not happen, or at least not as they had envisioned. This is when you need to be patient and reflect on everything that has happened. Usually, we miss out on many insights because we were expecting something flashy. Just because these insights are quieter than expected doesn't make them less valuable.

Ayahuasca is getting to know you, and the first night is much like a first date. Take it slow and treat the entire weekend as an opportunity to deepen your relationship with grandmother. You made it through the first night; now it's time to reflect, relax, and recalibrate for the second night. Crawl into your ceremonial cocoon and prepare for the rest of the weekend.

Rest and Reflection

An ayahuasca experience is an energetic one. More often than not, it will be one of the most intense encounters in your life. While you might be eager to see what the next night brings, adequate rest is necessary. Being well-rested and hydrated is recommended even the night before the ceremony begins. After the first night, this becomes even more important. While you can simply rest during this period, you can also try a specific yoga pose that might help even more.

This is known as *savasana* (corpse pose), where you lie completely still. You might wonder why this pose is a part of yoga, which is all about different kinds of mindful movement. The practice of yoga understands the importance of resting the body after an intense session. This pose is simple, yet many practitioners feel it can be the hardest to execute. This is primarily because we're not used to doing anything with our bodies.

Even though most of our movements might not be meaningful or productive, we still like to keep moving our bodies unless we're asleep. However, savasana has several benefits that should encourage you to try it.

When you've come out of an intense and physically exhausting session (be it yoga or an ayahuasca ceremony), this pose can help relax and rejuvenate you simultaneously. This is essential because not only do we want to give our bodies the rest they need, but we also want to increase our energy levels.

This pose has also reduced blood pressure levels, anxiety, and insomnia. After a session, you might still be left with residual anxiety. This can make it difficult for you to get a good night's sleep, which is important for the next session.

This posture requires us to lie flat on our backs, preferably on the floor. This is a surefire way of grounding our energy and connecting us to this material plane.

I like to do this pose outside in nature, under a tree, or on the beach. Grounding in nature boosts the benefits of this pose and allows the body to recharge using the natural healing energies of the elements. This posture gives us the kind of rest that helps repair our tissues and heal the body on a deeper level. This means that our bodies get time to bask in the good parts of the ceremony.

Here's how you can practice this position.

The first thing to do is to lie flat on your back. You should not use pillows or cushions for this purpose. If you feel very uncomfortable, consider placing a small cushion below your neck. Make sure your legs are comfortably placed in a way that is slightly apart from each other. Your arms should be placed along your body without touching it. Again, be as relaxed as possible, and make sure your palms are facing upward. Now, close your eyes.

After this, you can start breathing and bringing awareness to different body parts. Start with your toes and say silently, "toes relax." Visually move up your body, stopping at each body part until you reach the top of your head and relaxing each muscle and organ along the way. As you breathe in, let your body be rejuvenated. As you exhale, let all the exhaustion leave your body. This is an unhurried pose, so don't try to rush anything. You should feel your body getting lighter as you let go of all the stress and tension plaguing you.

You don't need to be anywhere but here. Do this for at least 15-20 minutes to relax your body and mind completely. After 20 minutes, roll over to your right side, curl up like a baby, and stay in that position for the next couple of minutes. Remember, in this and other poses, you should avoid sudden movements as much as possible. After some time, you can get up with the support of your right hand on the floor and stay in a comfortable position.

Take gentle breaths as you slowly open your eyes again and ease back into this world.

Some of us might come out of the ceremony feeling like we can conquer the world. Depending on the visions you see or the healing that takes place, you might notice a positive aura surrounding you. This is amazing, but it doesn't mean you should undertake physical or mental strenuous activities immediately after the ceremony. You might be in a hurry to integrate with your daily life, but that's usually not a good idea. So, what should you spend your time and energy on?

We come back to reflection. If you've gotten into the habit of keeping a journal, this will help you during this period. You might not remember everything from the journey you've just undertaken. However, there might be some things that stood out for you. Try to note some of the most amazing experiences you've had and the darkest emotions or reactions you remember.

Mindfulness will help you observe these events without any judgment attached to them. A simple thing you can do is to write down what you saw and how it made you feel. Some of these images can be disturbing, but when you write about them in a detached state, you might begin to understand some of their hidden meanings. You can also add questions where you like. For example, if you see a particular image and don't quite understand what it means, you can note it and set your intention for the next night accordingly. Remember, you don't need to obsess over anything you've witnessed. Writing will help you channel your energy away from obsessive thoughts. If you don't feel like writing, you might want to make a voice recording of yourself reflecting on the evening and aspects you would like to remember.

You might find yourself extremely sensitive to external stimuli, so the best thing to do is focus on and nurture your inner self during this period.

Reading and Inspiration

On the second day, I like to bring a spiritual book to read that helps root my experience in something sacred (I have recommended a few at the end of this book). You will be very sensitive after the first night, so be mindful of who you speak with and your conversations. You will notice a heightened sensitivity to people's energies in the group. Respect your intuitions and steer clear of anyone sucking your energy—you need to recharge and honor your own needs.

Many people will ask you how your journey was. This is a difficult question, and only some people are prepared to describe the depth of their journey when the ceremony ends. I had one experience where, once the ceremony ended, I couldn't speak for hours. Honor whatever the medicine has brought you and relax into the subtle energies that embrace you after the ceremony.

Discussing your experience with others may feel tempting, but you should wait until the integration circle to gather your thoughts and feelings. There is no right or wrong way—follow your heart and intuition. If you hear someone talking about having a vision or seeing a spectacular set of images, realize that everyone dances with ayahuasca differently. Your experience is unique to you, and medicine works on various dimensional levels of your being. Be careful not to compare or diminish your experience when you hear others talking about theirs. While listening to other people's experiences is essential, it would be far more helpful if you could understand how these experiences have helped them.

The main thing is that you should feel confident and inspired enough to proceed to the next stage of the journey.

Dieta Review

If you've been restricting yourself in the days leading up to the ceremony, you might feel eager to resume your regular diet. While this makes sense, it's not recommended. If you're about to go for the second night of the ayahuasca ceremony, it's especially risky to return to your regular diet. Not only will it create uncomfortable sensations during the ceremony, but your entire experience might get interrupted.

Even if you're going back to your life after the first night (but you are going to stay for the second night, right?), retreats recommend that the *dieta* should be adhered to for as long as possible, and certainly for a week after the ceremony. This is because your body is undergoing energetic shifts even after the ceremony. These effects can manifest in cycles. You might experience emotional highs, while at other times, you may feel hopeless and sad for no reason. These energies will take some time to settle, and you need to reintegrate into your life slowly.

Since most of our regular diet conflicts with what is appropriate for an ayahuasca experience, rushing back to it might cause purging episodes. Therefore, try to slowly ease into your previous diet over the course of the next few weeks.

Now, we're ready to experience the second night of ayahuasca. After this, we'll move into the most important phase of integration.

Five

Toward Integration

Letting go of the negatively charged energies surrounding life issues, when stimulated energetically through healing practices, is a way to maximize the effects of those therapies and to begin to break the vibrational chain that would continue to magnetize to you experiences of similar vibration.

~ *Oneness*, Rasha

Many people who work extensively with ayahuasca and other psychedelics believe that the real work begins after the ceremony. This might sound weird to those who have long anticipated the ceremony. After all, isn't the process of ingesting the sacred brew the whole point? Well, yes and no.

We need ayahuasca to help take our lives in a new direction. Ayahuasca is a medium through which we can come into contact with our deepest fears and biggest blockages while also understanding what can truly make us happy. However, an ayahuasca experience does not provide us with an instruction manual for the rest of our lives. The best thing it does is it shines a light on those parts of our lives hidden from us. What we do with that information is completely up to us.

This is also why practices such as meditation and reflection are encouraged as part of the preparation for our journey. Not only do these practices help us during the ceremony, but they have a significant impact on how this ceremony affects our lives later.

In this chapter, we'll talk about why integration is necessary, the different elements of integration, and how we can integrate these two extraordinary nights into our daily lives.

What is Integration?

Integration is the process of making sense of our experiences with ayahuasca and using those insights to recreate our lives. Most people understand that integration is a part of the ayahuasca experience, even though we don't know what it truly encompasses. There are a few reasons for this.

First, as I mentioned, there can be an extreme emphasis on ayahuasca use as an end rather than a means to an end. This is likely propagated by people who go to these ceremonies as a part of their edgy or adventurous lifestyles or those who go purely for recreational purposes. People need to understand that ayahuasca has never been meant for reckless use. Yes, the experience can be joyful and beautiful, but its significance doesn't end at the ceremony.

Second, many people don't set intentions before the ceremony, so they struggle to understand what they witness during the encounter. When you don't know why you came here in the first place, all you will be left with in the end is confusion and a vague sense of having gone through something important. This is more frustrating than never having experienced ayahuasca in the first place.

Third, we are primarily a result-oriented society. Even when it comes to profoundly spiritual or therapeutic practices, we simply don't have the patience to see the work through. This is reflected in our impatience with the ceremony itself, where if we don't have confounding and earth-shattering experiences immediately, the ceremony might as well be a failure.

Take the example of another practice, such as tarot reading. Anyone who has worked with tarot for years knows its primary purpose is to sharpen your intuition. It can provide you with a path, give you hints, and even provide you with hope. However, it's not a divination tool because it gives you definite answers about your future. A good tarot reader will leave you with more questions about yourself and your path than answers. Frustrating? Maybe, but only because we don't understand how the Divine Source works. The same goes for an ayahuasca experience. It tells us that there's more work to do, which makes most of us stop dead in our tracks.

Therefore, you first need to stop considering integration as another item on your checklist. There might be retreats that pay much attention to integration, but even the best ones usually don't do much beyond forming integration circles (more on this soon). Integration can be difficult. What helps me settle during integration are swims in the ocean, walks in nature, music, reading, meditation, art, and reaching out to my friends from the retreat.

Let's explore why we need to integrate. What are the feelings and concerns we're left with after the ceremony?

Why Should We Integrate?

Throughout this book, we've looked at Indigenous practices so that we can understand the core beliefs behind these ceremonies. In contrast, many things find a parallel in ancient rituals. Integration (at least as we know it) might not be one of them. Surprised? It's true; many shamans don't lead integration circles per se. People are encouraged to make sense of their experiences in solitude if they wish.

Those who want to discuss their experiences usually form small groups and talk about what they have experienced.

If they believe they should take some specific actions as individuals or as a community, they do so without making a fuss about it. In other words, the day after an ayahuasca ceremony might look eerily normal to outsiders.

Does this mean integration is a superficial westernized concept? It might be westernized, but it's not superficial. Let me explain. In most Indigenous societies, ayahuasca is woven into the fabric of their daily life. It's a part of their most important customs, healing and divination, and other rituals. These communities live in communion with nature. They understand and revere the plant as a spiritual being and find themselves fortunate for having known its secrets. Also, because they know how to live in harmony with other plants and animals, they have a stronger sense of self than most of us. They're traditionally away from the many scourges of modern society. While they have deep knowledge and wisdom amongst them (the wisdom that is shared and celebrated), they also live their lives according to these principles. What I mean is they already apply a lot of this knowledge to their daily lives.

These communities don't resist spiritual or mystical visions; they welcome them. When a message comes across to them in these ceremonies, they don't spend hours questioning it. They know they need to act on it; they even know how to act on it. In Indigenous communities, ayahuasca is already *integrated* into their lives. There is no disconnect, no confusion, and certainly no *unlearning* required.

This is different for most of us. Because we've spent our lives dissociated from ourselves, disconnected from nature, and discontented with everything possible, we treat this experience more as a shock than a blessing. We realize that we have months, possibly years, of work to do before we can fully understand our true selves. Another reason that makes integration important for most of us is that we're not used to accepting things without spending hours and days analyzing them. Don't get me wrong; many benefits come primarily from left-brained thinking.

However, we sometimes lose our intuition in the process. We want to be convinced about everything using logic and reason. Thus, in many ways, integration offers us an opportunity to think about what we've felt. We want to understand our experience in an almost clinical manner. Thankfully, this process does lead to a greater appreciation and cultivation of our inner instincts.

Possible Scenarios After the Ceremony

The first thing to understand is that you will feel raw for a few days after the ceremony. Take it slow, and don't make any snap decisions. Give yourself some extra room to ease back into your routine. The afterglow of the ceremony is attractive and powerful. If you felt connected to someone from the retreat, be mindful of that connection and give that new relationship some space to breathe.

Everyone has a unique experience with the ceremony. However, there are a few different kinds of issues and roadblocks many of us face after it. Let's explore some in detail.

Scenario 1: "The ceremony has brought up a lot of difficult emotions and traumas, and I have no idea how to deal with them."

You might feel scattered if you've experienced an ego death during this ceremony. Okay, that might be an understatement. Chances are, you might be feeling lost and overwhelmed. Remember what we said about our ego acting as our defense mechanism? We feel we're left alone now that it's been stripped away. Also, remember that these feelings don't only revolve around what has happened to you but also your role in your own and other people's lives.

Accountability is a bitter pill to swallow. When you remember everything about your past, you also get reacquainted with shame, guilt, anger, fear, and inadequacy surrounding these experiences.

In some extreme cases, we might also have encounters that affect our mental health. Sometimes, this might be because the ceremony wasn't conducted with empathy and understanding. Other times, the experiences we have might be too powerful or disturbing for us to be able to cope with them. While these instances are rare, it's important to check in with yourself to understand if you need professional help.

These emotions don't go away after the ceremony and might even be intensified when we're taken out of the context of a healing space. If you feel raw and uncertain, reach out to the ceremony facilitator or book a session with someone who can help you understand your feelings.

Scenario 2: "The world as I've always known it has changed dramatically. How do I navigate through it? How do I create a space for myself again?"

Chances are that you decided to undergo an ayahuasca ceremony because you had become too comfortable in your current life. You wanted to shake things up; however, things may have gone too far. It's a bit like the COVID-19 pandemic. While the optimists want to believe that there's a lot of potential for change and regeneration (and some even think this can lead to the creation of a better world), most of us find ourselves reeling from the way things seemed to have changed overnight.

In the case of ayahuasca, things might change overnight. Why do we hold on to things, jobs, and relationships that stopped working for us a long time ago? Because they make life easier or keep us from doing the hard work of integrating into our new lives.

The problem with ayahuasca is that it does not give you the luxury of ignoring the changes you see around you. What's more, these changes aren't of the world as much as they reflect the changes within you. Now you have no option but to create new routines and different ways of moving through this world.

Scenario 3: "I've never felt lonelier in my life. It feels like no one understands me anymore."

One of the reasons that it's so difficult to return to your old life is that your experience is not the norm. As I mentioned earlier, Indigenous societies thrive on the fact that these ceremonies, by nature, are community-driven. While the popularity of ayahuasca ceremonies has grown considerably in the West, there is still a lack of widespread acceptance regarding them.

Since the substance itself is illegal, these ceremonies are usually held discreetly. The only places that can afford to advertise operate in legal countries or through specific permissions. This means you can't openly discuss this ceremony with anyone you don't trust fully. Second, even if you confide in someone, you might feel judged by those who don't understand your reasons for participating in the ceremony.

Our society is already more fractured and isolated, not to mention polarized, than ever before. An ayahuasca experience might not be what brings us closer unless there's more acceptance of these practices.

Even if you're lucky enough to have people who support you and understand your need to pursue this path, they might not necessarily be in a position to discuss the topic with you. This experience is largely ineffable. You can't put it into words and be satisfied with what comes out. Even if you do, it will be like speaking in a foreign language with your friend or partner. This is also why many people wish to do these ceremonies with a close friend or partner.

So, you desperately crave support and community but feel misunderstood and alone. What do you do? I recommend talking with someone from your ceremony about any challenges that you might be experiencing. Many medicine communities offer online support groups—joining these groups offers a way to share privately with like-minded individuals.

Scenario 4: "I don't understand my experience at all. I suppose it is profound, but what is the point if I cannot make sense of it?"

This might happen. Sometimes, all we get out of an experience are images and visions that might carry some significance, but we don't get it yet. Maybe we need more sessions to understand these visions. Maybe we need to do additional work related to healing, like meditation, breathwork, or journaling. Sometimes, we might even need to see a psychoanalyst or someone adept at interpreting dreams.

It is possible that we might not find any easy answers or interpretations and that the only way to make sense of all this is to develop our intuition. Admittedly, this can be one of the hardest things to do when you already feel you need clarification.

Scenario 5: "I want to preserve this feeling I've had since the ceremony. How do I hang on to this?"

This is, in many ways, the opposite of feeling

disconnected and confused. Also known as the afterglow, this is a common experience that most people have after an ayahuasca ceremony. During this period, people find themselves connected to everything and everyone in the world. They might experience empathy for all living beings and feel unconditional love.

This state might resemble the blissful state that comes with achieving mindfulness or a higher level of meditation. During this phase, people might find that their worries and concerns have evaporated, and they feel less burdened by the past. They also feel less anxious about the future and start believing in a plan more significant than themselves.

This is especially true in the case of visions. Some visions are so transformative that everything makes sense to the participant. However, the problem with this feeling is that it doesn't seem to last. In some cases, people feel the positive effects of the ceremonies for years afterward. For example, many people believe they have never felt as free of depression or stress as they did after the ceremony. For some people, these feelings return after some time, but a lucky few see long-lasting changes. While more research is needed in this field, there is merit in exploring whether these effects can be prolonged.

While we cannot do much in terms of clinical research, we might still want to find ways to hang on to this beautiful feeling. Otherwise, the entire experience seems futile. Even though another ceremony can give us similar feelings, it wouldn't make much difference if those feelings were also transient.

Scenario 6: "The experience taught me a lot; it showed me where my issues stemmed from and areas I could improve upon. Where do I go from here?"

Many of us come from an ayahuasca experience feeling particularly encouraged. The encounter shows us the relationships that don't serve us anymore. It also makes us realize that we're clinging to old patterns and habits out of fear or inertia. Moreover, it makes us believe that a new reality is possible. However, it doesn't give us what we would call solutions.

It's not like our problems are suddenly solved, or our relationships are now working for us. Yes, we have a new perspective on life, but we still need to apply these learnings practically. When we return to our real lives, we still need to take accountability for our actions.

How do we put everything we've learned so far together to create the life we now know is possible? We'll explore some possible answers in the next chapter.

Six

Integration Process & Methods

Integration happens only with integrity and honesty towards others and oneself. When we have finally let go of all excuses and lies, and have taken responsibility for our lives, guilt disappears.

~ Ayahuasca, Javier Regueiro

While there is no set path that everyone needs to follow as part of their integration, there are a few broad categories that most of these steps belong to:

- taking accountability for the areas of your life that need to be taken care of

- understanding your true self

- fulfilling your soul purpose

I'm not saying that all three categories apply to each of us. Neither are these the only steps that can apply to you. However, these are common to most people.

Accountability

This is the hardest of all things you need to do. First, you must ensure that you stick to the *dieta* for as long as possible. In general, see which parts of your pre-ceremony routine you can stick to. You won't like all of it. You won't even resonate with some of it. That's okay. However, there are parts of this routine you might now enjoy. For example, if you used to love your morning walks in nature, try to find time for them after the ceremony. Similarly, if you find that eating less processed food agrees with you and you don't crave it anymore, try to stick with your new lifestyle. This is especially important because we sometimes decide that we can let these behaviors or habits go for some time, only to find out that it's difficult to build them again.

The second aspect of accountability is much more challenging. Here, you need to address the issues and concerns that have been nagging you for a while but haven't been addressed. It is possible that you didn't know something was a roadblock in your life until the ceremony, but now that you know, it's up to you to make sure you do something about it. It could be that a specific relationship needs healing. Or, maybe you have always been dissatisfied at work but now cannot bear the thought of walking into your office. Maybe you've been putting off something for years, thinking there will always be time to come to it later. This experience has taught you otherwise.

One thing to remember is that the ceremony itself cannot do the work for you. This is the perfect time to commit if you need to change your lifestyle. Write a vision statement incorporating the new behaviors or habits you want to see in your life. One exercise I like is imagining what a fantastic day in my life would look like. Next, I write in as much detail as possible about how that optimal day would unfold from when I wake up until I go to bed. Once you have that day written out, list areas you need to change to create that day every day.

None of these changes happen overnight. There are days when the work you need to do will feel impossible. You might ask yourself why you went to the ceremony in the first place. The success of the ceremony depends on whether you can show up each day for yourself and others. Each day you wake up is a new day to restart your life in the way you have imagined.

Understanding Your True Self

There is so much to us that we don't understand. A lot of it is hidden in our subconscious. The ceremony might have brought many of these parts to the surface. Everything that was previously hidden from us is now out in the open. This is the part where we heal ourselves and come to accept our true nature.

This doesn't start with acceptance. First, you reject everything you don't like (and trust me, there's a lot you won't like). Then, you reluctantly begin to face these parts of yourself and try to understand the reasons behind each trait. After much contemplation and conflict, you might begin to tolerate these aspects of your personality and soul, but there's still work to be done. You will try to heal what you can and let go of what you can't. Even though you might feel defensive during most of the process, you need to give yourself as much love and acceptance as possible. If you're generally kind, turn some of that kindness inward.

If not, take this as an opportunity to be more empathetic toward yourself and others. Ask yourself why you are so harsh to everyone around you. Learn to forgive yourself. Finally, you will be able to love all parts of yourself equally. Most of this work is known as *shadow work*. Ayahuasca is great at shining a bright light into our shadows.

As an example, you might have a lot of anger issues. The ceremony might have shown you this vividly and where some of these issues stem from. Maybe you could understand that you have been carrying the burden of intergenerational trauma. If you've always had a problematic relationship with your mother, you might not have paid attention to where some of her behavior stems from. If she was unusually strict or harsh with you, you might hold it against her, but now you know that her mother was even more strict with her. More importantly, you might understand that her behavior didn't come from any sense of cruelty. People who belong to this lineage might have wanted to protect their children.

It's difficult to understand where our parents' traumas came from. Sometimes, we might be the ones tasked with breaking this intergenerational curse. If the men in your family usually felt stifled or couldn't express their dreams, you can change the narrative. If the men faced a lot of traumas but weren't allowed to be open about their struggles, you could be the first to change the trend. The work I have done with ayahuasca has healed trauma in my lineage. I am eternally grateful for the opportunity to do this work, and it is an honor to share this possibility with you.

This intricate work of reckoning with yourself will result in immense rewards. When you know who you are, everything else becomes easier.

Fulfilling Your Soul's Purpose

It's rare for people to go through a spiritual experience without deciding to change at least some part of their lives. Some of us might not be drastically changing things, but we still have a new way of doing things. However, some of us find our true calling after a spiritual awakening. It might be a creative endeavor that we have been too scared to try earlier. Or, it might be something we had no idea we would enjoy. Usually, signs throughout our lives tell us what makes us truly happy. During an ayahuasca experience, these signs might be thrust into our faces, making them impossible to ignore. This is usually the point after which you're told that Spirit supports you in your dreams or leads you to something you love doing. For example, my partner's purge bucket turned into her long-unplayed saxophone during a ceremony, which led her back to a love of playing music. Ayahuasca introduces us to new opportunities and reminds us of who we used to be before we smothered our Spirits in trauma.

For some of us, however, the stakes might be higher. Our soul purpose might be connected to healing, teaching, and helping others on their path. While there's no hierarchy to these missions, you have a real opportunity to touch lives. You can help others who feel lost find their way back to themselves. This book manifests my desire to help others find their way to ayahuasca. It's not uncommon for people who the spirit of the sacred vine has touched to become a part of the plant medicine community. You might want to learn to heal, help others navigate these ceremonies, or even help people make sense of their lives after the ceremony. I am excited to see what awaits you on the other side of ayahuasca.

You might even want to touch people's lives in different, but no less powerful, ways. For instance, you could become an artist who gives hope to people through your work. You might want to become a writer to help others find a voice through your stories. Or, you could be attracted to activism, where you hold powerful people and organizations accountable and try to create a more equitable world.

Only you know if you have been called to take on a spiritual mission. If you are, have faith that you are protected on this path and that you can create a new world through your work. The spirit of grandmother will lead you back to the throne of your true self.

Methods of Integration

There are many ways to integrate yourself, and there are enough resources to help you with the problematic aspects of accountability. For example, mindfulness, meditation, trauma healing, dreamwork, developing your intuition, and communication techniques can help us at different stages of our integration process.

Here we will discuss some of the more common ones you can try.

Try Psychotherapy

You can try psychotherapy if you need to talk to a professional about your experiences and can afford it. Also known as counseling, this is a collaborative process where your therapist works with you to identify your behavior patterns and their causes. If your ayahuasca session has been primarily therapeutic, you will likely have a strong self-awareness. In this case, you can work with your therapist to discover tools and methods to help you overcome your destructive patterns.

A professional is your best bet if you've seen old wounds and past traumas resurface due to the ayahuasca session and feel the need to talk to someone about it. They will help you navigate difficult feelings and find ways to let go of the anger and pain that might come with them.

If you haven't received any specific visions or encounters to account for, but you feel a nagging sense of dissatisfaction regarding your life, a good therapist can help you uncover what lies beneath this discontent.

Psychotherapy is not helpful for everyone, but there's no harm in trying to understand yourself better through a professional's lens. I emphasize that not all therapists benefit you; some might even cause further harm by being insensitive to your needs. Therefore, you should do your due diligence before committing to anyone.

Have a Conversation with Loved Ones

I know this might be difficult, but there's a chance that your loved ones are equally worried about your state of mind. While they might not completely understand your experiences, they can certainly understand the results of those experiences. For example, if you feel you should move to a new place to study, work, or live, try explaining why this move might be important to those close to you.

If you want to change your career, give them reasons why

your current career is not working out for you. You may lose a few people on this journey. As painful as it seems, certain relationships are only meant to be a part of our lives for a short time. Usually, when we have learned our lessons, these connections die a natural death. In some cases, the end might be more brutal, but it's still necessary.

You might find many friends and family members drifting away when you begin a new path. This can be painful, but you should feel grateful for what these relationships did for you. Those that stay will usually be very interested in supporting you on this new path. Ask for help when needed.

Attend an Integration Circle

As we've seen, these psychedelic experiences can often feel very lonely in their aftermath. Even the most well-intentioned people in our lives might not be able to offer us the perspective and support we need, primarily because we exist in two different worlds (in a sense) in the aftermath. In these situations, an integration circle can come to our rescue.

While most retreats offer these integration circles as part of their package, they might need more. Also, we might need to be a part of these circles more than once to get the support we truly need. Therefore, it's best to find integration circles that are local to where you live. If you cannot find them, you should try starting one independently.

What is an integration circle? It's a group of people who have had psychedelic experiences and want to share them in a nonjudgmental space. As it turns out, the only ones who won't judge us are those who have gone through similar experiences. Here, you can explain your visions in detail, try to communicate their meanings, and describe how you feel after having gone through them.

Since this is a safe space, you can also recount any troubling situations that have arisen due to this ceremony. You can talk about your traumas (as much as you're comfortable), difficulties navigating reality, and any other doubts you might have. You might even inspire someone else to share their story.

There are different kinds of integration circles. You can choose the type that you're most comfortable with. For example, you might choose a circle where a facilitator or guide leads the group. These are very helpful if you are a beginner because there is usually more structure to these sessions. Also, you might be able to direct specific questions to the therapist.

However, some people prefer to be a part of peer-led groups because it seems more intimate and less hierarchical. Since everyone has the experience to share and no one is leading the group, more people might open up without hesitation. At the same time, the discussions here can be relatively free-flowing, and it might take some time for you to make sense of things.

In the same way, some people love the idea of online sessions, especially because it offers accessibility that is not found elsewhere. People who cannot visit physical locations or are not too keen on meeting people physically, at least in the beginning, can find online classes amazing. As with everything else, though, in-person sessions tend to be much more intimate. Since the entire ayahuasca journey is one of energy, it helps when we can sense other people's energy in the same space. It's similar to the experience of the ceremony itself. During these circles, you can meet people, hold hands, sing and dance in the same space, and even hug someone if you feel comfortable. Physical interactions are usually more meaningful, so you should seek them out if possible.

These integration circles have immense benefits. Even if you're uncomfortable talking about your specific experience, you can always just listen and feel like you belong somewhere. Many people form deep bonds and lifelong friendships through these circles, and these bonds come from a place of understanding and empathy rather than more superficial concerns. Group therapy is also helpful for those of us who struggle with accountability. We'll be prompted to do the needed work when we see others going through similar experiences and trying to make the best of them.

However, it must be emphasized that any group-based session cannot replace the work that needs to be done individually. You should see integration circles as one of many aspects of your work. These work best in support of individual therapy or healing work. (See the resources section at the end of this book for more information on working one-on-one with someone qualified to help you through integration.)

Find Your Community

An integration circle is a great way to find your community. Even beyond this, you can actively lookup resources that help people who have gone through different psychedelic experiences. Even though the psychedelic community in the West is getting larger, it's still not enough for everyone to get the support they need from a single group. You can always start at the retreat. Try to keep in touch with people you like and feel comfortable talking to. Try to start your community if possible. Another way to do this is by finding people who are doing spiritual or therapeutic work.

This can often be a lonely and confusing experience, so you need to actively try to find others who might be seeking companions on this journey.

Now that we've learned about integration, let's consider other factors before deciding if you want to participate in another ayahuasca ceremony.

Seven

After Ceremony

Ceremony allows you to release the energies, programming, and beliefs that are preventing you from living your fullest potential.

–*The Ultimate Guide to Shamanism*, Rebecca Keating

Now that you've returned from the ceremony, you must consider a few things. We've already discussed how you should start and maintain your integration process, but there are a few other things to keep in mind.

Returning to the Ceremony

If you've had a fantastic experience, you will most likely want to return to the feelings you've experienced. Even if you didn't have a great experience, you might be curious to know if there's more to it than what you saw and felt. Some people get encouraged by the changes they see in themselves after the ceremony and want more insights about their inner selves. These are all good reasons for trying ayahuasca again.

However, some might wonder if you can get addicted to ayahuasca. After all, when you feel like experiencing something again and again, how do you know if it's because you have experienced a profound spiritual or therapeutic connection or because you have gotten used to the high, you might experience during a ceremony? After all, isn't that similar to an addiction to other drugs?

Clinically speaking, no evidence exists that people can develop a tolerance to ayahuasca. This means that, as of now, there's an extremely low risk of developing an addiction to this brew. However, this doesn't mean you cannot get psychologically addicted to the drug. By this, I mean that you might convince yourself that ayahuasca ceremonies are the only way to heal or understand yourself better.

I understand why you might think that. The people who have seen the positive effects of ayahuasca on their mental health can swear that nothing else even comes close. Some people equate one night spent with ayahuasca to years of therapy. When the anecdotal evidence is so promising, one can't be blamed for wanting to be a part of this miracle. However, we already know that your experience does not have to mimic anyone else's experiences with the vine.

There is a high probability that all sessions will also differ for you. So, if you think you had a fantastic experience this time, there's no guarantee that the same thing will happen again. This doesn't mean that you might not come across visions or feelings you have encountered before; it simply means that you shouldn't bet on it. Return to the ceremony when you're ready to surrender or if you feel called. Only you will know the right time and cadence of your healing.

However, you should refrain from jumping from one ceremony to another because of the integration process. As mentioned in the last chapter, most of the work begins after you have participated in the ceremony. This process of integration isn't over the morning after the ceremony. It might take months to assimilate everything we've learned and put it into practice. Sometimes, we need to learn new skills to ensure we reach our new goals—quite often, this takes time.

If you find yourself keener on the ceremony than the work that needs to come afterward, you should return to your intentions. Additionally, if you use the ceremony to escape your current reality, that's not a good idea. More often than not, the ceremony will make you come face-to-face with everything you've been running from.

This is not to say that you should not consider returning to the ceremony; many believe you will get more benefits once you become more comfortable with the vine. However, always be honest about why you want to do so. If you have good reasons to go back and can manage your expectations, then return. I hope you have a meaningful experience when you do. In my particular case, I get called back frequently, and I honor that call wholeheartedly.

Life Changes

When you return from the ceremony, the first couple of weeks can be the hardest in terms of getting reacquainted with your life. While it's rare, some people can experience the effects of ayahuasca even a week after returning. This usually includes purging, but it might also include experiencing altered states of consciousness.

This means you might suddenly feel on a different plane of existence. You can also have visions or out-of-body experiences in certain extreme cases. This is why it's important to spend time at home or in a safe space for some time after a ceremony. The best thing you can do is spend time resting or soaking yourself in nature. You can also do relaxing activities with loved ones. It's recommended that you have people you can trust, just in case you have an experience and feel unmoored from reality. You can also spend time soothing your senses during this period. Be mindful that you will likely have a heightened sensitivity to many sensations at the time, so try not to overwhelm yourself with anything. Ease back into your regular life, and give yourself ample time to rest and reflect.

Another thing to remember is that you should be able to

reach out to your retreat center or facilitator if you experience something out of the ordinary after returning home. While your friends and family members can comfort you, they might need more help in terms of actual information and solutions. The person who should be able to explain things to you, including why you might be having a particular reaction to the experience, is your facilitator. Additionally, hiring a therapist or coach who understands how ayahuasca works (and ideally has experience with ayahuasca) is always helpful.

Press Pause

I've talked about the importance of taking time to self-reflect after returning from the ceremony. Your integration process should include moments of self-reflection and work with people who can help you define priorities and goals in your new life.

However, all of this comes with a caveat. When I say "new life," I don't mean that everything necessary before the ceremony will become meaningless. Neither am I telling you to throw your old life away for a new one. Just as you will be sensitive to external stimuli at this time, so, too, will you find yourself in a different state of mind. You might have an extra burst of energy, a passion for achieving everything on your wish list, and a reduced tolerance for those you think aren't aligning with your new path. This is what we call a ceremonial *afterglow*.

The first couple of weeks is usually when you experience

the most intense afterglow of the ceremony. I'm not saying that this is misplaced. Maybe whatever you think needs to change is real. Maybe your concerns are spot on. Maybe you finally have the clarity you need regarding your relationships. None of this has to be false, but it can be way more intense than needed. Consequently, your actions might become more drastic than required. We sometimes need drastic actions to help us make fundamental changes. One of my friends, after a ceremony, knew that he had to leave his wife and make a major change—he told me the details the day after the ceremony. It took him five months to take the actions prompted by ayahuasca in that ceremony; a little drastic action would have saved him a ton of suffering.

This behavior isn't exclusive to a psychedelic experience. Have you ever felt so excited at a prospect that you forgot to do your due diligence? Have you ever fallen head over heels for someone and thrown caution to the wind? Similarly, have you quit a job in the heat of the moment without making a backup plan? We're all prone to making rash decisions when we're under immense pressure or feel extremely bored with our lives. Sometimes, this works out, and sometimes it doesn't. Rasha reminds us in *Oneness* that every action and non-action is part of our chosen path: "There is nothing that you are capable of being different from—for all of it is your creation. Your life is a living reflection of your vibrational essence."

As crucial as our instincts are in making decisions, we cannot base all our decisions solely on what we feel in the moment. More importantly, most of us don't have the kind of instincts that we should be proud of. It takes time to sharpen our intuition and make balanced decisions.

The integration process doesn't ask us to act first and think later. The more time you take to think and reflect on your decisions, the better your chances of creating a life that holds meaning. Wait a few weeks, talk to people you trust, journal, and reflect on your feelings. If, after self-reflection, you still feel like you should make the changes you feel strongly about, then go ahead.

Sometimes, you will know something is so right in the center of your heart of hearts that you won't need any reflection. When you have that feeling, trust it and take action.

Conclusion

If you're reading this book, you felt drawn to participating in an ayahuasca ceremony. Maybe you have friends who have participated in their ceremonies, or you've read accounts of people who have benefited immensely. Maybe you've heard from a famous person that ayahuasca has changed their lives unimaginably. Maybe you want to see what all the fuss is about finally.

There's nothing wrong with being curious. You should always seek knowledge, especially about things otherwise alien to you. If you've picked up the book only to understand what ayahuasca ceremonies look like or what one can expect from them, by all means, do so. However, there's a good chance you will be more interested in the ceremony than you had previously thought. This is usually how it works with psychedelics and ayahuasca in particular.

So, what if you've been considering participating in a ceremony yourself? Most likely, you would be excited and nervous in equal measure. You might find yourself surrounded by numerous questions. Where should I take part in the ceremony? Who should I contact? Who should I turn to for advice? What are the things to keep in mind when participating in the ceremony? What do I need to do in terms of preparation? How much preparation is too much preparation?

However, before you go on to these questions, consider other questions. These might not seem directly related to the ceremony but bear with me. First, have you been discontented with how your life is going? Most of us will answer yes, but you should dig deeper. What are the areas of your life that you feel the most dissatisfied with? Are the specific issues new, or have they always been at the back of your mind? If so, why do you think they've become so important right now?

These are difficult questions, and you should focus on them only a little. I understand that, but I would still want you to try. Not only are these questions important for you to determine whether you want to participate in the ceremony, but they will also help you prepare for the ceremony in case you decide to go.

These questions will form the basis of your intentions. When you ask yourself these questions, you should also ask whether you've tried other methods to help you with your feelings. If not, why? If yes, then ask yourself why they haven't worked for you. This is important for you to determine why this particular approach will work better than others. Are you trying to go to a ceremony because everything else has failed? Or is it because you think certain parts of your psyche cannot be addressed through more conventional methods?

By now, you must know what is not working for you and why you want to try different approaches. There is another question to ask yourself at this point. Are you trying to run away from your current life? Or are you trying to change it for the better? Will this ceremony make things easier for you once you go back? Or do you expect things to get harder after the ceremony?

There is no right or wrong answer, but there are honest and dishonest ones. You don't need to convince me or anyone else that you are the right fit for an ayahuasca ceremony. No criterion in the world can determine that. The only thing you need to do is understand the true motivations behind your interest in this experience.

Let's try a slightly different approach. What if I gave you some answers or suggestions of what you can expect from the ceremony? What if I told you that the ceremony would have its highs, but it will also have its lows? Also, what if both the highs and lows are equally intense? What if there is a possibility of you having an experience that is primarily boring or even difficult? What if you come back feeling exceptionally sensitive to everything?

What if, instead of feeling more connected with the world, you feel intensely alone after the ceremony? What if you have all this energy but don't know where to put it? What if you feel like your entire world has turned upside down? If my questions have left you a little breathless— good; you're now getting some sense of what the ceremony (or its aftermath) might feel like.

What if I told you that, no matter what you're expecting from the ceremony, you'll most likely have an experience you are not prepared for? These questions aren't meant to scare you away; they're meant to help you understand whether you'll be able to undertake this journey or not. Before you make your decision, you will likely read blogs, articles, and books like this to understand better what to expect from your ayahuasca experience.

You might even watch videos that help you prepare for the journey ahead. You might follow all the rules, do everything that is asked of you, and research as much as possible. While all of that is essential, even necessary, to help you navigate this experience, more is needed. Ayahuasca has a spirit that is all her own. She's the only one who can decide whether you should be communicated with and how. You will also direct the experience, but only to the extent that a vessel makes itself available for energy to flow through it.

If I try to glamorize this experience or make it look an exciting way of spending your time, I will be doing you a disservice. Instead, I will ask you if you want to do the hard work. Are you willing to go through this experience without any specific expectations? Are you willing to surrender to whatever happens, especially if it's dark and unpleasant? Are you going to immerse yourself in these experiences and not shy away when things get difficult?

This ceremony might test you in ways you do not expect. Don't get me wrong; I don't mean that your experiences will only be unpleasant. There's a good chance that you will be a part of something so amazing and euphoric that everything else will pale in comparison. If you think that good experiences cannot be challenging, you've not had one on ayahuasca.

When you return from a challenging experience, you might not know how to care for yourself or do the healing work necessary to let go of these emotions. You might even struggle with anger, shame, and self-loathing. Your trust in people can also be shaken. This makes sense, as difficult as it might be. However, what do you do when you have a fantastic experience?

What if you experience beautiful visions that show you the beauty of this and other worlds? What if you have an emotional experience where you can forgive someone else and find peace within yourself? What if you see the true nature of this world, and your heart fills with unconditional love? What if you return from this experience with expanded consciousness and a better understanding of your higher purpose? Will things get easier?

In many ways, it might get harder. There are enough people worldwide who are nursing their wounds and coping with their traumas. While everyone might still need to be ready to do the work, you will likely find enough support from others if you confide in them. However, very few people are spiritually exalted and believe in spreading light to other beings. You are here to change that.

Are you a lightworker? Would you want to become someone who sees the light in everybody, even those who don't see it in themselves?

Will you carry the lightness of love through the burden of life? Some of these questions need to be more abstract. Some of them seem extremely far-fetched as well. That said, nothing is more abstract and concrete than the experience you're about to have. It will simultaneously feel like the only real thing in the world and the wildest dream ever.

These questions will help you understand whether you're ready for the ceremony. Remember, the decision to participate in this ceremony should be yours and yours alone. Nothing should persuade you to do so, not even this book. And, even if you have the right intentions and want to solve your problems once and for all, don't expect ayahuasca to do that for you. No amount of ayahuasca in the world can take the place of your actions and decisions. Ayahuasca isn't a panacea for your ills, it is a doorway to self-knowledge, and for me, it has been the greatest gift of life.

If you're willing to push the boundaries of what you've always known and expand your consciousness, if you want to meet all of yourself, and if you want to start redefining your life, you are more than welcome to be a part of this journey. This book is an effort to make you feel less alone on this path, to make you understand that your trials and tribulations are as much a milestone as your successes, and to tell you that it's okay not to know things sometimes. Are you ready to manifest into the unknown? This book will not give you all the answers but will help you form the right questions to direct your life.

In the end, I would like to mention certain things. First, you should always consult your doctor and prioritize your health when dealing with any major changes in your lifestyle or undertaking a psychedelic journey. No matter how exciting things might look, and no matter how badly you want to get on the other side of this experience—*nothing is worth compromising your mental or physical health*. Second, choose safe environments to be vulnerable in. If possible, go for your first experience with someone you trust. If nothing else, you will have peace of mind that you're not going through this alone. Third, always respect the vine and understand that you're a part of something deeply spiritual that holds a lot of meaning to Indigenous communities. Consider yourself fortunate to be able to partake in this experience and make the most of it with deep gratitude and an open heart.

***

If you are still trying to figure out how to move forward with plant medicine and you require further guidance or coaching, I offer confidential initiation and integration counseling via Aya101.com to either help prepare you for your first journey or to assist in the integration process.

Haux. Haux.

Glossary

- **Ayahuasca:** Plant-based psychedelic tea. Also called *iowaska, yajé, 17oage, vegetal, natema, uni,* or *caapi.* It's made from the bark and stem of the *Banisteriopsis caapi* vine, along with other ingredients.

- *Ayahuasqueros*: Shamans who serve ayahuasca and care for people during a ceremony.

- **Decoction**: A liquor, especially from a plant, that is made by boiling a substance.

- **Dietas**: Preparation for an ayahuasca ceremony where certain foods and behaviors are modified to honor the spirit of ayahuasca.

- **DMT:** N-dimethyltryptamine is a hallucinogenic tryptamine entheogen found in ayahuasca.

- **Icaros:** Songs and prayers sung by shamans to honor the spirit and call for protection during an ayahuasca ceremony.

- **Limbic system**: The part of our brain responsible for our emotional and behavioral responses.

- **Monoamine Oxidase Inhibitor (MAOI)**: Prevents the primary psychoactive ingredient in ayahuasca (DMT) from breaking down in the digestive tract.

- **Pachamama:** Usually translated as Mother Earth. A more literal translation would be "World Mother" (in the Aymara and Quechua languages). The Inca goddess can be referred to in multiple ways, the primary way being Pachamama. Other names for her are Mama Pacha, La Pachamama, and Mother Earth.

- **Psychoactive**: Refers to drugs or substances that significantly impact our thoughts, feelings, or behaviors.

- **Serotonin**: A chemical found in our brain, blood, and gut that transmits messages between the brain's nerve cells and affects various body functions.

- **Shaman**: A priest or priestess works with mystical energies to guide, heal, and connect with the Divine.

- **Syncretic**: Anything that combines different beliefs or schools of thought.

- **Tyramine**: An amine derived from tyrosine that simulates the working of our sympathetic nervous system.

- **Visual cortex**: The part of the brain's cerebral cortex that is responsible for processing visual information.

Acknowledgments

I am deeply grateful for plant medicine, and the healing humanity receives from this majestic spirit. Thank you, plant medicine. I want to thank my teachers, Natascha, Zan, Cesar, Veronica, and Ascentia, for their loving guidance and dedication to my healing. Thank you to the Indigenous peoples who have kept these magical plant traditions alive and available. On my journey, the divine presence of Buddha, Saraswati, Ganesha, Hanuman, Durga, Kali, Lakshmi, Sekhmet, Ra, Horus, and Kuan Yin have blessed my path—so much gratitude for the ancient traditions and sacred teaching.

Thank you to my loving partner, Mar, for supporting my crazy journey and being a beacon of love, understanding, and kindness. Thank you to my ceremony brothers and sisters who have traveled by my side and sat through long nights and deep wounds while we all held each other lovingly with empathy.

Thank you to the seen and unseen spirits, my star family, the dragon and the snake, the jaguar and the condor, the cobra and the hummingbird, the phoenix and the rhinoceros, to sacred geometry, to the creator, and Divine Source. Thank you to my heart for recognizing and leading me back toward the Source.

References

Alex, A. (2020a, May 31). *Ayahuasca Book "The Cosmic Serpent" by Jeremy Narby.* Ayahuasca Timeline - From Mythic Origins to Global Popularity. https://ayahuasca-timeline.kahpi.net/jeremy-narby-cosmic-serpent-ayahuasca/

Alex, A. (2020b, May 31). *DMT: The Spirit Molecule Book Ignited Psychedelic Culture.* Ayahuasca Timeline - From Mythic Origins to Global Popularity. https://ayahuasca-timeline.kahpi.net/2000-dmt-the-spirit-molecule-book-is-published/

Alex, A. (2020c, June 3). *Richard Spruce's Colorful Encounter with Ayahuasca in 1851.* Ayahuasca Timeline - From Mythic Origins to Global Popularity. https://ayahuasca-timeline.kahpi.net/richard-spruce-ayahuasca-amazon/

Ayahuasca Ceremony History and Origins. (2019, January 30). Spirit Vine Ayahuasca Retreat Center. https://spiritvineretreats.com/ayahuasca-blog/ayahuasca-ceremony-history-and-origins/

Ayahuasca Retreat Preparation- Recommendation Guide. (2021, August 21). Nimea Kaya Retreat Center.

https://www.nimeakaya.org/ayahuasca-retreat-preparation/

Ayahuasca Quotes (43 quotes). (2022). Goodreads. https://www.goodreads.com/quotes/tag/ayahuasca

Barker, S. A. (2018, August 6). N, N-Dimethyltryptamine (DMT), an Endogenous Hallucinogen: Past, Present, and Future Research to Determine Its Role and Function. *Frontiers in Neuroscience*, 12. https://doi.org/10.3389/fnins.2018.00536

Bezrutczyk, D. (2022, September 14). *Ayahuasca Addiction and Abuse.* Addiction Center. https://www.addictioncenter.com/drugs/hallucinogens/ayahuasca/

Fernando, G. I. (2016, June). Ayahuasca: Friend or Foe? *American Journal of Psychiatry Residents' Journal*, 11(6), 13–13. https://doi.org/10.1176/appi.ajp-rj.2016.110605

Frecska, E., Bokor, P., & Winkelman, M. (2016, March 2). The Therapeutic Potentials of Ayahuasca: Possible Effects against Various Diseases of Civilization. *Frontiers in Pharmacology*, 7. https://doi.org/10.3389/fphar.2016.00035

French, S. (2021, December 13). *What happens when you go to an ayahuasca retreat? A first-timer's guide.* New York Post.

https://nypost.com/article/ayahuasca-retreat-first-timer-guide-experience/

5 Ways To Prepare For Your Ayahuasca Retreat. (2019, January 14). Soul Quest Retreat Center Orlando. https://www.ayahuascachurches.org/5-ways-to-prepare-for-your-ayahuasca-retreat/

Fresh, P. (2022, January 4). *A Long, Strange Trip: Magic Mushrooms, MDMA, and the Promise of Psychedelic-Assisted Therapy.* WebMD. https://www.webmd.com/mental-health/story/psychedelic-assisted-therapy

Halley, C. (2021, September 29). *The Colonization of the Ayahuasca Experience.* JSTOR Daily. https://daily.jstor.org/the-colonization-of-the-ayahuasca-experience/

Hamill, J., Hallak, J., Dursun, S. M., & Baker, G. (2019, January 7). Ayahuasca: Psychological and Physiologic Effects, Pharmacology and Potential Uses in Addiction and Mental Illness. *Current Neuropharmacology, 17*(2), 108–128. https://doi.org/10.2174/1570159x166661801250 95902

Hudson, J. E. H. (2020, January 21). *How Can You Drink Ayahuasca Legally in the U.S.?* Chacruna. https://chacruna.net/how-can-you-drink-ayahuasca-legally-in-the-u-s/

Deciding to take Ayahuasca. (2022, July 12). ICEERS. https://www.iceers.org/interested-taking-ayahuasca/

Kat, A. (2019, March 10). *Trauma healing with ayahuasca and breathwork—a personal journey.* BBTR Institute. https://www.biodynamicbreath.com/news/trauma-healing-ayahuasca-breathwork%E2%80%8A-%E2%80%8Aa-personal-journey/

Kehoe, D. (2022, July 27). *What Is Ayahuasca? Uses, Experience, Effects and Dangers.* The Recovery Village Drug and Alcohol Rehab. https://www.therecoveryvillage.com/ayahuasca-addiction/

Leonard, J. (2020, January 31). *What to know about ayahuasca.* Medical News Today. https://www.medicalnewstoday.com/articles/ayahuasca#benefits

Liana, L. (2021a, February 3). *How to Choose an Ideal Ayahuasca Shaman, Facilitator or Retreat Center.* EntheoNation. Retrieved September 7, 2022, from https://entheonation.com/blog/choose-ideal-ayahuasca-facilitator-retreat-center/

Liana, L. (2021b, November 25). *The Uncensored Guide to Preparing for Ayahuasca Ceremony.* EntheoNation. Retrieved September 7, 2022, from https://entheonation.com/blog/ayahuasca-ceremony-preparation-dieta/

Merriam-Webster. (n.d.). Decoction. In *Merriam-Webster.com dictionary.* https://www.merriam-webster.com

Merriam-Webster. (n.d.). Limbic system. In *Merriam-Webster.com dictionary.* https://www.merriam-webster.com

Merriam-Webster. (n.d.). Psychoactive. In *Merriam-Webster.com dictionary.* https://www.merriam-webster.com

Merriam-Webster. (n.d.). Serotonin. In *Merriam-Webster.com dictionary.* https://www.merriam-webster.com

Merriam-Webster. (n.d.). Shaman. In *Merriam-Webster.com dictionary.* https://www.merriam-webster.com

Merriam-Webster. (n.d.). Syncretic. In *Merriam-Webster.com dictionary.* https://www.merriam-webster.com

Merriam-Webster. (n.d.). Tyramine. In *Merriam-Webster.com dictionary.* https://www.merriam-webster.com

Merriam-Webster. (n.d.). Visual cortex. In *Merriam-Webster.com dictionary.* https://www.merriam-webster.com

Nichols, D. E. (2016). Psychedelics. *Pharmacological Reviews*, 68(2), 264–355. https://doi.org/10.1124/pr.115.011478

On Integration. (2019, February 8). Ayahuasca Wisdom. https://ayahuascawisdom.com/integrating-ayahuasca/

Recommendations. (2018, September 4). Ayahuasca Foundation. https://www.ayahuascafoundation.org/healing/preparation/ayahuasca-ceremony-preparation/

Reyzer, R. (2022, January 21). *The 2-Night Ayahuasca Experience Report*. Rafal Reyzer. https://rafalreyzer.com/the-2-night-ayahuasca-experience-report/

Serotonin syndrome - Symptoms and causes. (2022, January 22). Mayo Clinic. https://www.mayoclinic.org/diseases-conditions/serotonin-syndrome/symptoms-causes/syc-20354758

Szetela, A. (2017, February 19). *Ayahuasca, meditation and activism: On cultivating the mindful politics of love*. Salon. https://www.salon.com/2017/02/19/ayahuasca-meditation-and-activism-on-cultivating-the-mindful-politics-of-love/

Tanev, M. (2021, December 26). *How Do Psychedelic Integration Circles Work – and Can I Start One?* EntheoNation. https://entheonation.com/blog/psychedelic-integration-circles/

Tanev, M. (2022, August 16). *The Ayahuasca Diet: What Is It and Why Do It?* Psychable. https://psychable.com/ayahuasca/the-ayahuasca-diet-what-is-it-and-why-do-it/#:%7E:text=A%20healthy%20diet%20before%20the,salt%2C%20spices%2C%20and%20sugar

Savasana - Corpse Pose. (2022, February 6). Art of Living (India). https://www.artofliving.org/in-en/yoga/yoga-poses/shavasana-corpse-pose

What is a dieta? (2008, March 28). Ayahuasca.com. http://www.ayahuasca.com/psyche/shamanism/what-is-a-dieta/

White, J. (2021, March 15). *5 Tips for Navigating a Difficult Ayahuasca Experience.* NewLifeAyahuasca. https://www.newlifeayahuasca.com/post/5-tips-for-navigating-a-difficult-ayahuasca-experience#:%7E:text=BREATHE,responding%20to%20pain%20and%20emotion

Woodrow, C. (2022, May 3). *How Ayahuasca Changed My Life.* Ordinary Traveler.

https://ordinarytraveler.com/how-ayahuasca-changed-my-life

Woolfe, S. (2022, August 15). *What is Ayahuasca Integration and Why is it Crucial?* Healing Maps. https://healingmaps.com/what-is-ayahuasca-integration/

Recommended Reading

Agni Yoga Society. *Heart*. Agni Yoga Society, 2017.

Blavatsky, H.P. *The Secret Doctrine*. Theosophical Press, 1888.

Campos, Don Jose. *The Shaman & Ayahuasca: Journeys To Sacred Realms*. Studio City: Divine Arts, 2011.

Dass, Ram. *Be Here Now*. Harmony, 1978.

Farrand, Thomas. *Shakti Mantras: Tapping into the Great Goddess Energy Within*. Ballantine Book, 2003

Founder, Christian. *Grandmother Ayahuasca: Plant Medicine and the Psychedelic Brain*. Rochester: Park Street Press, 2021.

Fronsdal, Gil. *Dhammapada*. Boston, Shambhala, 2006.

Gorman, Peter. *Ayahuasca in My Blood: 25 Years of Medicine Dreaming*. Gorman Bench Press, 2010.

Krishnamurti, Jiddu. *First & Last Freedom*. New York: Haper Collins, 1954.

Maharaj, Nisargadatta. *I Am That*. The Acorn Press, 2012.

McKenna, Terence. *Food of the Gods: The Search for the Original Tree of Knowledge*. New York: Bantam Books, 1992.

O'Reilly, James. *Ayahuasca: Soul Medicine of the Amazon*. James O'Reilly, 2016.

Pinchbeck, Daniel and Rokhlin, Sophia. *When Plants Dream*. London, Watkins Media Limited 2019.

Rasha. *Oneness*. Santa Fe: Earthstar Press, 2003.

Regueiro, Javier. *Ayahuasca: Soul Medicine of the Amazon*. Lifestyle Entrepreneurs Press, 2019.

Strassman, M.D., Rick. *DMT Spirit Molecule: A Doctor's Revolutionary Research Into the Biology of Near-Death and Mystical Experiences*. Rochester: Park Street Press, 2001.

Watts, Alan. *The Way Of Zen*. Vintage, 1999.

Resources

Medicine Music

https://soundcloud.com/derek-dodds-581667106/sets/la-ceremonia-sagrado-de

Podcasts

Tim Ferris #523: Dennis McKenna — The Depths of Ayahuasca: 500+ Sessions, Fundamentals, Advanced Topics, Science, Churches, Learnings, Warnings, and Beyond
https://tim.blog/2021/07/21/dennis-mckenna/

Joe Rogan #1854: Rick Strassman
https://open.spotify.com/episode/56jFEMXBynPmREm463zRVc

Youtube Videos

Dr. Gabor Maté on Trauma, Addiction, Ayahuasca, and More
https://youtu.be/H9B5mYfBPlY

Aubrey Marcus: Ayahuasca With "The Dragon of The Jungle"
https://youtu.be/Va9idaJNLyw

Websites

Multidisciplinary Association for Psychedelic Studies
https://maps.org/ayahuasca/

The International Center for Ethnobotanical Education
https://www.iceers.org/ayahuasca-basic-info/

About the Author

Derek studied Vedanta in Varanasi, India, and Buddhism at Kopan Monastery in Kathmandu, Nepal. He served as a trustee of The Krishnamurti Foundation of America for over a decade while promoting Krishamurti's work through print and digital media. Derek has a master's degree in public policy & administration.

Derek's first experience with Ayahuasca occurred in Peru's sacred valley near Machu Picchu in 2003. He has been working with plant medicine for twenty years and has a deep meditation practice. He offers initiation and integration counseling via Aya101.com.

AWAKEN
PUBLICATIONS

Awaken Publications is dedicated to helping humanity awaken higher states of consciousness through a deep exploration of oneself. Awaken Publications focuses on ancient traditions and cultures' spiritual and sacred teachings. To see a list of our upcoming titles exploring healing modalities, sacred art, energy work, and plant medicines, open your favorite browser and click awakenpublications.com. If you want to get in touch with one of our authors, please email us at this email: awakenpress@gmail.com.

May all beings be peaceful.

May all beings be happy.

May all beings be safe.

May all beings awaken to the light of their true nature.

May all beings be free.

Printed in Great Britain
by Amazon

23565992R00106